Bird

on
Basketball

How-to Strategies
from the Great Celtics Champion

Updated and Revised Edition

Larry Bird

with **John Bischoff**

Addison-Wesley Publishing Company

Reading, Massachusetts ▪ Menlo Park, California
New York ▪ Don Mills, Ontario ▪ Wokingham, England
Amsterdam ▪ Bonn ▪ Sydney ▪ Singapore ▪ Tokyo ▪ Madrid
San Juan ▪ Paris ▪ Seoul ▪ Milan ▪ Mexico City ▪ Taipei

Library of Congress Cataloging in Publication Data

Bird, Larry, 1956–
  Bird on basketball.

  Bibliography: p.
  Includes index.
  1. Basketball.   2. Bird, Larry, 1956–
  3. Basketball players—United States—Biography.
I. Bischoff, John.   II. Title.
GV885.B544   1986   796.32′3′0924[B]   86-22209
ISBN: 0-201-14209-0

Originally published in 1983 as *Larry Bird's Basketball: Birdwise*
by the Phoenix Projects, Terre Haute, IN.

Photo Credits: Cover photos by Dick Raphael; first picture of color
insert—*Sports Illustrated* photo by Toney Tomsic; second and
third insert photos—*Sports Illustrated* photos by Peter Read
Miller; fourth insert photo—*Sports Illustrated* photo by Richard
Mackson; fifth insert photo—Dick Raphael; rear cover photo—
Dick Raphael. All other credits as noted.

Design and illustrations: Paul Henrichs
Cover design by Marshall Henrichs
Set in 10-point Helvetica

6 7 8 9 10-CRS-9897969594
Sixth printing, November 1994

ACKNOWLEDGEMENTS

Thanks to the Boston Celtic organization. I would also like to thank Mary Ann McQuillan for the teaching, Cathy Fouty and John Obst for the reading, Ward "Dina" Hubbard for two titles, Don Swan for many things, and others who made this publication possible.

CONTENTS

Photo by Dick Raphael

This book is dedicated to the parents
who make everything possible.
Mrs. Georgia Bird
and Mr. and Mrs. John J. Bischoff

Two figures move about a playground basketball goal. One is 6'9", the other 6'3".

Rubber soles scratch at grit covering the 40-foot-square concrete slab. A leather ball *thump-thumps* against the hard surface, then lazily arches toward the cylinder. *Thump-thumps* and arches. *Thump-thumps. . .*

"We called it 'hoops,' played for 'pops' on Hubbard's court in Deerfield Subdivision, and invented a 'hot dog' version of 'Horse' we called 'Showtime.'" The smaller of the two says this to the larger of the two.

"We played here, mostly. Mike and Mark and me. We played two-on-one. Mark was biggest. Pretended he was Walton."

The players begin a game of "Horse." The greater one flips his wrists from 25 feet out. The ball angles up, then down. It sits down in the net with a softness somehow tangible. Rope cord snap is muffled by humid air.

"I was there when you did your thing at State. Great. That last season was a dream come true for basketball fans. I've never seen so many people so excited for so long about one thing."

"Yeah, people up there, around here, I guess all over Indiana are nuts about it. Basketball, I mean. It's just a game. But they do."

The smaller one tries to fool the larger one with a shot he's saved up. He drives around under and behind the basket, arcs his arm, and hooks it over the bank board. It goes in.

"It's the small towns. People need heroes. They need to be for something. You know the year you took Springs Valley into the playoffs, 1974. Over a million Hoosiers attended the state tournament games that year. It's just a game, but somehow important. It's a part of the culture here."

"I guess."

"You know somebody told me something about you. A sportscaster, I won't mention his name, told me he talked with you after you lost the final game against 'Magic' and Michigan State. He told me you couldn't believe the whole thing, winning the tournament, was so important to all those fans. He said you said that if you'd known you could have maybe done something, something extra, to win that championship game. But I sure don't know what else you could have done."

The bigger player misses the over-the-bank-board shot. He says nothing.

"You know, when we were in high school, we even set up our own summer league, with uniforms and everything. We painted a red, white, and blue half circle at the back edge of the court and brushed in a red *D*, blue *B*, and white *A*. It stood for the Deerfield Basketball Association. The big rivalry was between the Deerfield Dukes and the Youngstown YUMs. I was a YUM."

The 6'9" one, who is Larry Bird, shoots an underhand scoop shot from 10 feet that barely moves the net. He still says nothing.

"We played all the time. Just like you played all the time. None of us made it as far as you. How come?"

"You gotta put it all together. A lot of players work on shooting. But there's a lot more to the game. You've gotta take the game apart. Break it up into pieces. And work real hard to polish those little pieces. Like rebounding isn't just going up for the ball. There's a lot to it. You've gotta learn to anticipate the shot. You've gotta learn how the ball comes off the rim. How to position yourself. And there's a lot more."

"So if I'd broken my game down, and known what you know about the game, I'd be playing in the NBA this season."

"No. Nothing personal. The odds—about three hundred players out of over two hundred million in the U.S. play in the NBA—are against you. You've got to have something special, be lucky to make it. But even if you can't play in the NBA, you can learn to play your best and have a lot of fun. That's what's most important about basketball: it's fun."

As the smaller one takes another shot, the day is dying. The two figures are now shadows, one 6'9", the other 6'3". It is still hot, at least 90 degrees. And cicadas whine unseen up in the green summer trees. The only other sound is the *thump-thump* of the ball.

"One more game?"

"Yeah."

The two play one more, and then another, using the silhouette of the net against the evening sky to sight their shots.

John R Bischoff

INTRODUCTION

The year is 1993. The story below is fiction based upon facts known at this time. The names have not been changed to protect the innocent.

Fade in: Wide-angle view from the top of the Boston Garden. Fans are filing into the stands. The Boston Celtics and Philadelphia 76ers are at their respective goals shooting warmup shots.

ANNOUNCER:
Nineteen, count them, nineteen championship flags hang here in the ancient Boston Garden, where today CBS will bring you the contest between the Philadelphia 76ers and the Boston Celtics.

But the game isn't our story today. Both teams have clinched playoff berths. And it's not the classic confrontation between fierce rivals that will stir emotions. Because this is the end of an era. This is the final regular-season appearance of one Larry Joe Bird, perhaps the single greatest player in the history of the game.

Cut to historic highlight film of Larry Bird's career.

ANNOUNCER:
It's hard to believe fourteen years are gone since he first slipped on Celtic green. It's hard to believe the rags-to-riches, Horatio Alger, American success story came true for the once self-proclaimed "hick from French Lick." It's hard to believe the Indiana country boy came to the big city and polished his game until it shone like a newly minted coin. It's hard to believe the man too slow to do the things he does won't be out on the parquet doing them next year. It's hard to believe.

Cut to graphic of Larry Bird's career stats.

ANNOUNCER:
What's easy is to look back over the years and say Larry Bird was the most complete basketball player ever. The level line of the stats is solid evidence. Averaging 22 to 28 points per game each season, close to 800 rebounds each year, around 500 assists each year—for fourteen years the most well-rounded numbers in the league. And five world titles make another thing easy, to say he was a winner. Down-to-the-wire finishes and the Celts need a basket to win, a steal to get the chance, a rebound to seal it. Who? Him. When? In the nick of time. The corn-fed Sir Lancelot with shock-of-wheat hair would come in on alabaster legs to save the day.

Fade in: Floor-level shot showing Larry in an empty gym after practice, shooting, practicing his fakes, etc.

ANNOUNCER:
Another thing that's easy, though not revealed in numbers, is to say he was more than a great basketball player. He was and is a great individual. Ask any player with whom he played. Ask any coach. They'll tell you he was the best teammate you could have. They'll say he was a coach's dream. Because he didn't lead by getting out in front. He led from within the team, through his example, with his innate ability to make the next best move on the hardwood chessboard. Because he gave the team what it needed when it needed it. No more. His play made other players look better than they were.

It's easy to look back now and say these things. It's in the books. But earlier this week we visited with the man who knew most of the Bird story before it unfolded. The sage, the seer of roundball, drafted Larry in 1978 when he was a junior with a year of college ball to play. He was eligible for the draft because he was red-shirted his freshman year. 'Seventy-eight then was his official graduation year. But Red would wait until '79 for his Bird.

Cut to floor-level shot of Red Auerbach sitting in a folding chair at center court of the Boston Garden.

ANNOUNCER:
Mr. Boston Celtic, Red Auerbach, did you think Larry Bird would turn out as good as he did?

AUERBACH:
I knew he would be good. But who could know he'd turn out like he did? It's a credit to his determination. To see Larry Bird perform has been one of the great thrills of my life. He's the consummate professional. You can study him from a hundred different angles and you'll still be missing something. He never quit trying to improve himself. After practice everyone else would hit the showers, but he'd be out there running extra laps. "I'm gonna run three miles," he'd say. Or, "I'm gonna shoot a hundred, maybe a hundred and fifty free throws."

ANNOUNCER:
What do you think Larry's greatest accomplishment was?

AUERBACH:
That's a tough one. There were so many great moments. But I think he made his "bones" in the '83–'84 championship series. I mean after that series there was no doubt about his abilities, about his leadership.

It was a bruising series. New York first. Then Milwaukee. Then L.A. They were the "greyhounds." Big, quick, strong. Magic Johnson, Kareem, McAdoo, Worthy, and the rest were favored. And in the first three games they looked like they might just blow past the Celts without breaking stride. Boston's game two win was a fluke. And in the third the Lakers reeled off 137 points to Boston's 104 to hand them their worst drubbing in playoff history.

Enter Larry Bird. Larry hadn't been silent in the first three games. He'd been getting his stats. But something was missing. The intensity wasn't there. In the team, I mean. So it was after the blowout he says this to the press, "We played like a bunch of sissies today." He said it and nobody believed it. But it's something I would have done, too. He was willing to take the risk that his teammates would turn on him. He made a calculated move to stir them up.

And, of course, the sissies became the bullies. They fought back and won one that maybe talentwise they shouldn't have. But that team had Larry Bird averaging 27.4 points a game and grabbing 98 rebounds in the championship to lead all players.

ANNOUNCER:
So in your mind, motivating the team in that series was his greatest challenge, his greatest success?

AUERBACH:
No, I didn't say that exactly. It was a turning point. His greatest challenge is coming up. The afternoon's coming when the sun's gonna shine through those grimy windows up there. It's gonna fall on those nineteen banners. It's gonna fall on Russell, Cousy, Havlicek, and the others. That afternoon number 33 is going up with the rest of them. When it does, you're gonna have 15,000-plus pairs of watery eyes up there in the stands. You're gonna have 15,000-plus hearts in throats. And I'll tell you something else, mine's gonna be one of them.

ANNOUNCER:
I'll tell you something. Officially he may be hanging it up, but for those of us who love the game he'll always be out there, diving into the wood for the ball, flipping deadly passes, faking one, two, three times, and putting the ball up soft as cotton over the rim.

It is unusual, but I think fitting, for us to focus our pre-game show on one player. But the impact of Larry Bird's accomplishments may not even be fully appreciated for years to come.

We have with us Bob Ryan, former sportswriter with the *Boston Globe*, now analyst with CBS, to answer the question that needs to be asked at this time, one argued in living rooms and bars across the country: Is Larry Bird the greatest basketball player of all time?

RYAN:
You really know how to put a guy on the spot.

Before anyone makes a decision about greatness and who is the greatest of all time, he should take a stroll through the Boston Garden. I did, before I made my decision.

Standing in the midst of all that history, among the ghosts of all those great players and championship teams, you get a spooky feeling when you start talking about Larry

Bird's place in history. The problem is compounded when you throw into consideration the likes of Kareem, Oscar, Jerry West, even George Mikan, and others—the great non-Celtic claimants to the title "greatest."

It makes you want to be very careful and very sure when you make your pronouncement. Look at the situation of Mickey Mantle and Babe Ruth. In his time, Mantle was called the greatest, inheritor of the title from the "Babe." But through all these years I think Babe Ruth looms very large in the long view—maybe because his position in the history of the game allowed for greater impact. Everyone else came after and invited comparison only in his day, nostalgia putting him back in his place after a few years.

But the statistics remain cold and hard. Larry has the best all-around statistics. Other players scored more points—Kareem. Other players had larger totals of assists, rebounds, and so on. Other players led their teams to more championships—Bill Russell and so on. But if you want to talk about the player who did the most of *all* these things, who do you come back to?

And if you want to talk about impact on the game. Before Bird entered the league, the game was in decline. NBA was synonymous with selfish one-on-one play. Media coverage was more likely focusing on contract disputes and drug use than excellence of play. And that changed.

Fans began to turn out in throngs to see the unselfish player who was more interested in winning than in compiling stats. They came to see a professional who hustled every minute he was on the court. The league saw the attendance figures bulge wherever Larry touched ground. They took notice. Teams became teams again. Passing was back in their vocabulary for the first time since Cousy.

And perhaps the extent of his impact could best be judged by his effect on the game in its natural state. Larry Bird became the tag most honored on sandlots around the world. It replaced "The Pistol" and "The Doctor."

So am I going to say it? I don't know if it's my place. Besides, it's already been said, sometime ago by one who should know. In '82 the great Bob Cousy said with an earnest smile upon his face, "Everybody is going to say it in five years, but I'm going to say it now. Larry Bird is the best player to ever play this foolish game."

It is a familiar setting to even the most casual of basketball fans. A brilliant Sunday afternoon in late spring. Boston Garden. The odd-looking floor and the World Championship banners. This is the second game against the Chicago Bulls in the opening round of the 1986 playoffs. The Celtics, who finished the regular season with the best record in the league, have won the first game of the series and would desperately like to win today before they must play game three in Chicago.

It is obvious from the outset that this will be a special game. Chicago's Michael Jordan is dazzling. Each time down the court he defies the laws of gravity, seeming to climb through the air, gliding toward another two points. He will set a record this day with 64 points in the most awesome scoring display in NBA playoff history.

But Jordan and the Bulls are destined to lose. While Jordan is writing his name in the record book, forward Larry Bird is quietly orchestrating a Celtics victory. Bird's 36 points, 12 rebounds, and 8 assists will somehow be lost in the rush to chronicle Jordan's performance. In the end, it will be Bird's ability to bring himself and the entire Celtics team to progressively higher levels of play that will be the true difference. It is a phenomenon that can be described as the Bird Effect.

The game is in its second overtime period. Fatigue is showing on the faces of the players. Normal shots become Herculean efforts. It is the time in a game when most players prefer that the ball be anywhere but in their hands.

The Celtics are clinging to a 133–131 lead in the final minute of the game. As the Bulls come down the court, Jordan somehow becomes wide open 12 feet from the basket. As he releases his shot, 15,000 mouths go dry. He misses. Robert Parish, the Celtics center, gathers in the rebound and throws it to Larry Bird.

"Awkward" is a term often used to describe Bird as he dribbles the ball up court. In a game dominated by sheer grace and speed, Bird appears to lack both. As he rattles over half-court, a moment of anticipation flashes through the crowd and onto the court. There is a look of certainty on Bird's face. He heads toward the right side of the court, where Parish has positioned himself. It appears Bird is ready to shoot, to end the game as he has ended so many other games before, with his ever-so-soft jump shot floating an inch over the outstretched fingers of a defender. Bird cocks his elbows and knees and both Chicago defenders lunge toward him. At the millisecond of no return, just as the second defender, the man responsible for Parish commits toward Bird, the shot-to-be becomes a pass. Parish, completely undefended, scores the easy basket. The Celtics win. The Bird Effect.

Three weeks later, having disposed of the Bulls and the Atlanta Hawks, the Bird Effect was felt in Milwaukee.

The Celtics had jumped to a three-game lead against the Bucks in the best-of-seven Eastern Conference finals. It was the same Bucks team that in 1983 had dealt Bird and the Celtics their cruelest setback of the decade, sweeping the Celtics four games to none. It was now Boston's opportunity to return the favor.

The game was played in Milwaukee, a notoriously tough road date for most NBA teams. For three quarters, the Celtics and Bucks fought. The Celtics were clinging to a slim lead with five minutes left in the game when the Celts' starting guard, Dennis Johnson, fouled out. K. C. Jones, the Celtics coach, was now forced to move Bird to the guard position. The Celtics looked to be in trouble. The Bucks and their fans could sense the first blue sky after three games of rain.

Their mood changed quickly. Bird is a player with many tools to choose from, and on this occasion he decided the long-distance three-pointer would do nicely, thank you. Four times in a row Bird launched, and each time he found his mark. Each shot's psychological impact was far greater than its actual effect on the score. Bob Dylan's line "like a corkscrew to the heart" could have been written to describe the effect of each shot on the Bucks. The Bird Effect.

As the clock showed three seconds left, an incredible sequence occurred. The game was won, and Bird dribbled toward the corner of the court. As the clock showed one second, Bird picked up the ball and seemed to take a step toward the dressing room. But at the last possible instant before the buzzer sounded he turned and shot. As he released the ball, he continued off the court. He was halfway to the dressing room when the ball swished cleanly through the net.

Everyone from Santa Monica to Bunker Hill predicted that the 1986 NBA Championship Series would involve the Celtics and the Lakers for the third straight year. But someone forgot to let the Houston Rockets know they couldn't beat Los Angeles. Before you could say "Akeem Olajuwon," the Rockets had beaten the Lakers.

Boston won the first two games easily, but when the series went to Houston, the Celtics found out why Houston had beaten L.A. In game three, Houston came from behind to beat Boston. The play of the Rockets young tandem of 6'11" Olajuwon and 7'4" Ralph Sampson, dubbed "the Twin Towers," began to make the Celts wonder if indeed youth would be served.

Game four in Houston would be critical for both teams. A Celtics victory would place Houston in a three-games-to-one deficit—nearly impossible to come back from. A Houston victory would tie the series at two games. More important, it would establish Houston's momentum over the tiring Celtics veterans.

The game quickly took on the characteristics of an epic battle, each team trying mightily to deliver the blow that would break·the spirit of the opponent. The game would later be called the greatest in a decade.

With under three minutes left, the score was tied. The teams had been exchanging field goals, neither being able to establish more than a brief two-point margin before the other reciprocated. Bill Walton, the Celtics center, stood holding the ball 10 feet from the basket. Between him and two points stood a sea of white Houston jerseys.

For the entire game the Rockets had not allowed the ball to find Bird on the perimeter, where he has beaten many teams. Often as many as three Rockets would dash out to cloak Bird as soon as the ball headed his way. Given the success of the tactic, a less determined player would have conceded the position and looked for other options. Not Larry Bird.

For the first time all night, the weary Rockets stayed under the hoop, hanging on Walton. It was Houston coach Bill Fitch, a former Bird mentor, who first recognized what was about to happen. As the final Houston defender dropped toward the basket to help cover Walton, Bird made his move. Fitch waved wildly, like a signalman about to witness an unavoidable collision. Too late, the Houston defenders realized what was happening. Suddenly Bird appeared, 25 feet from the basket, wide open. Walton released the ball to Bird.

If you have ever experienced the eye of a hurricane, you would perhaps be able to describe the effect of the shot as it dropped through the basket. The deafening noise finally ceases. The fearful winds become dead calm. An eerie sense of peace sets in. Such was the feeling in Houston as the scoreboard registered three Celtics points, the final margin of victory, the Bird Effect.

The two days preceding Sunday, June 6, 1986, set local records in Boston for rainfall. The gloomy weather reflected the mood of most Bostonians well. Their beloved Celtics had returned home from Houston on Friday, humiliated by an ugly, one-sided defeat in game five at Houston on Thursday night. The game had suddenly erupted into a brawl during the second quarter. The Rockets' Ralph Sampson had instigated a fight that left the Houston team and crowd in a state of high emotion. The Celtics had uncharacteristically folded under the pressure and been dealt a lopsided defeat. Worse than the defeat were the questions being raised about the legendary "Celtics Pride."

By Sunday the weather had cleared. Bird, with no hint of swagger, vowed the Celtics would win the championship that afternoon. The Garden filled early, the faithful eager to witness the redemption.

That awful Thursday night in Houston, it had been the Rockets' ability to outrebound the Celtics that was the catalyst for their victory. Rebounding is basketball's free enterprise system, where hard work and determination are justly rewarded. Few teams can win without superior rebounding. It was only appropriate that the play that marked the end of the Rockets' chances in game six involved Larry Bird and a rebound.

Less than three minutes had been played. It is rare in basketball for a truly significant play to occur so early in the contest, but this would be an exception. Both teams looked tense; little had been established. The Celtics' Kevin McHale swooped in for any easy layup and the ball clattered around the rim and out. Robert Parish batted the ball back up and again it fell off the rim. The ball dropped to the right side of the basket where Bird stood. He wasn't alone. In front of the 6'9" Bird stood 6'11" Olajuwon, and behind Bird stood 7'4" Sampson. Bird shot straight up, his fingertips finding the ball at the apex of his leap, grasping it just before Sampson and Olajuwon could. As Bird descended, it became clear he would need to repeat his upward journey to score. He pumped his torso skyward, and Sampson and Olajuwon instinctively reacted, leaping at the same time, but Bird never left the ground. As the two Rockets blasted higher, Bird angled his shoulder between them and pushed the ball over the rim. The effect of the rebound and basket was enormous. Bird had sent a message that said, "You're going to have to fight me for everything."

The game turned immediately at that point in favor of the Celtics. They would go on to win by a huge margin, Bird scoring 29 points with 11 rebounds and 12 assists. After the game, as the Celtics celebrated their sixteenth World Championship, an elated Bill Walton was asked when he thought the championship was won. Nodding his head toward his exhausted teammate, he unhesitatingly answered, "The day Larry Bird was born!" Call it the Bird Effect.

WORLD ON A STRING

"He never holds it, just begins striding briskly down-court while the bouncing ball weaves itself intricately in and out of his legs...The basketball is his dancing partner, never causing Bird to reach for it or to break stride in any way."

John Papanek, Sports Illustrated, Nov. 9, 1981

Larry Bird, like other NBA stars, whips the basketball around the court as if it were a Yo-Yo whose string is wrapped around his middle finger. His hand casually waves "bye-bye" to the floor, and the leather globe rhythmically bounds back and forth between hand and floor. Whether he bolts downcourt on the fast break, or carefully picks his way through a gang of defenders, he commands the ball. It obediently returns to the hand of his choice, and is again sent off with new speed and direction. But thoughts of how high or how fast to dribble the ball don't clutter his mind. Dribbling, for Larry, has become an almost automatic bodily function. Like the beating of his heart, the bouncing of the basketball seems to regulate itself, and frees him to attend to the important business of searching for open teammates and shots.

Ten years ago you could have picked him out of any rag-bag assembly of sandlot players. Without seeing him shoot, pass, or rebound, you could have spotted a certain quality in the bearing of a young Larry Bird. His grace and poise, the ease with which he moved and handled the ball—they would have stood out against the rough background of a "shirts and skins" contest. It would have been impossible, at that early date, to guess at the round-ball success that would be his, but his "at home" manner with the ball would have been proof he had passed the game's first test. He had obviously fallen in love with the game, worked hard to master it, and sure enough had the physical ability and determination to play. You could have seen that the mixture of talent and desire were there; and that with a little more aging, might ferment into the "right stuff."

UPI/Bill Manning

Heads Up—*When dribbling the ball keep your head up with eyes on the court ahead. Here, Bird looks upcourt to find the open man. Notice, too that he's in a position similar to the ready stance, with knees bent and back straight. From this position he can easily pass off the dribble or move up-court with the ball.*

Cuddling it, spinning it on his finger, bouncing it off walls, dribbling it through the house, driving his mother crazy with it—always—the Bird and ball were inseparable. And today, when you see him move the ball upcourt like a guard; effortlessly fake and blow past his defender; sneak out of well-laid defensive traps; or smoothly glide into shooting position, you know the friendship remains unbroken. And, perhaps, more than any other, dribbling is the basketball fundamental responsible for the development of the special relationship between Larry Bird and the ball.

It's true that dribbling is just another subject on a basketball player's schedule, but it becomes more than a lesson when it is studied by the dedicated student. When a player spends as many hours practicing as Larry did, the lesson becomes the teacher. Dribbling practice brings the player into close contact with the ball. Out of that contact develops a feeling, an uncanny awareness of the ball. That's why Larry is a master of the game. He is in touch with the ball and so feels at home in the game. It shows in his fluid dribbling. It shows every time he handles the ball—when he shoots, passes, or rebounds. Even in overtime championship games against Philly, his relaxed control is intact.

And there's no doubt, when the game is on the line, the coach, the fans, his teammates, all want the ball in his hands. So does he. And when it's there, he's as happy as if he had the world on a string.

Learn to dribble with your head up and eyes looking straight ahead. This is the most important thing to learn about dribbling. If you dribble with your head down, you won't be able to see where you're going, and won't be able to see if your teammates are open for passes. Besides, there's no reason to look down. As coach Auerbach always said, "The ground is flat, the ball is round. You don't have to worry, it will always come back to your hand."

Another thing to remember is that the shot is your "big gun," the pass your "spear," and the dribble your "knife." You need to choose the best weapon for each situation. If you have a good shot, take it. If there's an open man ahead of you, pass it. There's no reason to dribble if you can shoot. There's no reason to dribble if you can pass. You can't dribble the ball to a spot quicker than you can pass it. Dribble when it's the only weapon you can use.

The dribble is your license to move the ball; however, you can only start and stop your dribble one time for each possession. So only use your dribble to get out of a defensive trap, move into shooting position, drive to the basket, or open a passing lane. Don't start dribbling unless it's going to do something for you. Don't stop dribbling until you can pass or shoot the ball.

You will find dribbling drills in the back of this chapter. Use them until dribbling comes as natural as walking down the street.

◁ **On The Move**—*As I drive around my man, I keep my eyes open for a teammate cutting to the basket. With the ball at waist height, I can easily make a flip pass off the dribble or continue my drive by pushing the ball out in front of me.*

Ball Control—*I have practiced my dribbling so I can control the ball at all times.*

Steve Cadrain Photo

Photo by Dick Raphael

The Protection Dribble—When you're tightly guarded, make sure you have the ball protected. Here, I keep my knees bent and my body low to the ground and positioned between my defender and the ball. My arm is extended to the floor, and I dribble the ball only a few inches off the floor. Notice too, that I propel the ball to the floor with just the snap of my wrist.

Photo by Dick Raphael

Photo by Dick Raphael

The Crossover—I execute a crossover step to move around my defender. I cross my right leg in front of my body and step around the left side of my defender. Notice that this move keeps my body between the defender and the ball.

The Speed Dribble—To move quickly downcourt on the fast break, I dribble the ball at waist height and push the ball out in front of me. I keep my head up so I can see teammates cutting to the basket, and defenders trying to steal the ball.

Steve Lingenfelter Photo

Driving—Before I drive to the basket, I keep my body between the ball and my opponent. From this position I use my peripheral vision to determine the defender's position.

Steve Lingenfelter Photo

When I'm sure I've got an open lane to the basket, I push the ball out farther ahead of me on a line to the basket. The ball will bounce up as high as my stomach or chest, but I always make sure my body is turned so my shoulders protect the ball.

Steve Lingenfelter Photo

The instant I think I can beat my opponent to the basket, I take off with a burst of speed. I push hard off my forward foot, and at the same time push the ball out in front of me. I dribble with my outside hand; my shoulders naturally protect the ball from the defender.

Steve Lingenfelter Photo

As I near the basket, I bring the ball up into shooting position with both hands to protect it until I release the shot.

Practice

The Figure 8—Before you begin dribbling, move the ball in, out, and around your legs in the pattern of the number eight. This exercise will give you a good feel for the ball.

Stop and go drill—Mark off four lines on the court about fifteen feet apart. If you're on a regulation court, use the existing lines; if you're on a concrete court, mark them off with a piece of chalk.

Start dribbling the ball, and walk to the first line. Stop walking, and dribble for five seconds. After counting to five, proceed to the next line. Move downcourt making sure to stop and count to five at each line. When you reach the end of the court, switch dribbling hands, and repeat the stop-start course in the opposite direction. As your dribbling improves, change your walking pace to a run.

The gauntlet—Set chairs in the middle of the court about ten feet apart. Start at one end, dribbling the ball with your right hand. As you approach the first chair (pretend it's a defensive man), keep your left leg back a little from your right. Change the angle of the ball so it travels close to your body, and hits the floor so it bounces up to your left hand. Dribble the ball to the next chair with your left hand. When you come to the next chair, change dribbling hands again. Repeat this pattern down the line of chairs. Make sure to angle your body so it's positioned between the hand you're switching the ball to and the chair (the defender). This is a good drill to help you learn to protect the ball while dribbling through traffic.

The Wheel—Use half the court for this drill. Pretend there's an imaginary x drawn on the court as shown below. Begin dribbling with your right hand, and move from position 1 to the center of the court. Pivot. Then proceed to position 2, still dribbling with your right hand. When you reach 2, pivot again, and change dribbling hands. Dribble with your left hand to position 3. Reverse pivot at position 3, and move to center court. Pivot. Proceed to position 4, still dribbling with your left hand. At position 4, pivot. Switch dribbling hands and move on to starting position 1. Repeat.▽

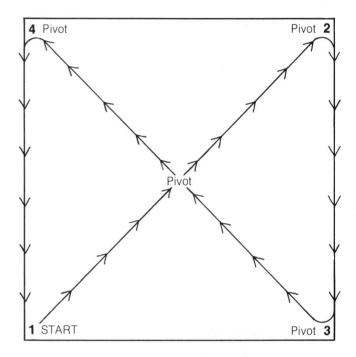

◁**Pass off the dribble**—You'll need to find a friend to help you with this drill. You should begin at position 1 and dribble to 2 at full speed. Your friend will start at position three and has the option of cutting to the basket and receiving a pass at position 4 or cutting to position 5 and getting the ball. He must make his move before you reach 2. When he makes his move hit him with a pass off the dribble at position 4 or 5.

The Speed Dribble—Dribble downcourt at full speed, and shoot a layup. Dribble the ball about waist high, and make sure to push the ball out in front of you three or four feet so you don't run into it.

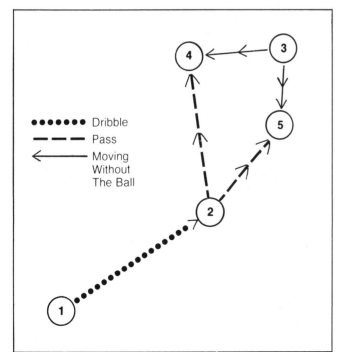

PASS FIRST, ASK QUESTIONS LATER

"Bird's passing was unselfish—and contagious. 'If you're open, he'll get you the ball,' Cowens noted. 'And he makes the other guys want to pass.'"

From The Pictorial History of the Boston Celtics by George Sullivan

The pass is a remarkable tool. Even in the hands of an amateur, it's the quickest, easiest way to shovel the ball from one player to another. But it does its most beautiful work in the hands of the skilled passer. With a deft snap of his wrists, the fine-fingered passer can pierce the heart of a defense and perch the ball on the edge of two points. Again and again his passes can find their way through the thorniest defense. The pass is his tool to cut the man-to-man apart—to split the zone. But zipping the ball around the court does more than destroy a defense. It makes an offense work.

A pass can be beautiful, important; however, it's worthless unless thrown to the right place, at the right time, with the right "touch". It can be fired quick, hard, and chest high, or lobbed slow, soft, and rim high; but should always drop in the shooter's hands like a cream puff; its placement requires only the flip of his wrists for the score.

That's asking a lot. But that's what a perfect scoring pass should be. And it's a shame most players are content to use the pass as a way to move the ball up court, play catch, or start an offensive play. The pass can be much more. Threading the ball through outstretched arms and legs, and sticking it in a shooter's hands is next door to two points. Another scores, but the passer feels the electric thrill of making it happen. Only a handful of players consistently experience the passer's reward. Larry Bird is, perhaps, the best of that small group. And it's the good passers, like Larry, and their appreciative coaches who understand that a player who develops and refines his passing skills is more important to a team than any thirty-point-a-game hotshot.

Bird goes up over the defender to pass the ball to a wide-open teammate under the basket.

Behind the Back—*Surrounded by defenders, Bird flips the ball over his shoulder to a teammate behind him.*

An imaginary game to fifteen by ones would do to show why this is true—why passing makes a team work. For instance, if teams were picked like this: one team with five terrific shooters, and one team with four average shooters and one Larry Bird—passing's vital importance would become clear by the end of the game.

First, of course, the teams would shoot for "outs." The "hot shots" would hit. The game would start with the ball in their hands. And it would go like this: right off, before the defensive machinery warmed up, the shooters would drill Bird's team. Before a drop of sweat had hit the floor, his team would be down 0-4.

Down by four points, Bird's team would finally go to work on defense. His players would get all over the shooters. The "hot shots" high powered offense would sputter a bit as the defense began taking away the easy shots. While on the other end, Bird would start to slip the ball around, over, and through the defense to this average shooters. And average is all they would need to be. His passes would hand them wide-open passes in close to the basket. Those shots would score, but a couple of twenty-five foot "bombs" by the opposition would keep Bird's team down 4-6.

Near the halfway point of the contest, the terrific shooters would be running around on the offensive end, desperately trying to get open for shots. But there wouldn't be anyone on the team to feed them crisp, accurate passes in good shooting position—just five guys looking to shoot. On the other end, Larry's teammates would be delighted to find the ball in their hands when they would need it, where they would need it. But even though his passing would make them work hard at getting open for passes, they would still do other things. Because they would be average shooters, they wouldn't expect to shoot the ball every time downcourt. They would set picks, look to pass to the open man, and work to get in offensive rebound position. Bird's players would mix their efforts together and begin to "cook." His team would jump into the lead 10-8.

It would get worse for the "hot shots." During time-outs they would start arguing with each other over who was—or wasn't— doing this or that. Each one would think he could single-handedly pull the game out for the team with his great shooting. Each one would be wrong. The every-man-for-himself style of play would not only weaken the shooters' offensive attack, but also destroy the fabric of cooperation that holds a team together and enables it to play good team defense. Of course, that would be great for Bird's

Looking for the Open Man—Here Dennis Johnson helps out by screening my opponent, Dominique Wilkins, as I look to pass.

team. His average shooters would find it easier to get open in their favorite shooting positions. Larry would find it easier to zip them the ball.

And all of a sudden it would happen. Bird's average shooters would be good percentage shooters. Larry's precise passing would regulate the kinds of shots they would get. His shooters would see how effective their team could be if they took only good shots, and realize that they had become better than average shooters. And because Larry's passing would be so contagious, his teammates would be looking for the open man. They, too, would be good passers. But best of all, because Bird's unselfish passing would unite the team in a spirit of cooperation, the four average shooters and one Larry Bird would be a team.

By the way, Bird's team would win the game 15-10. Passing would do that, too. It would make the team work.

Get the ball to the open man closest to the basket. That's your job on the offensive end. That's the only way you can win basketball games.

The reason is simple. Your team will have possession of the ball a given number of times in each game. That means you and your teammates will get only so many shots at the goal. Since teams usually get about the same number of shots at the basket, the team that takes the best shots will usually hit the most shots and win the game. Because it's easier to hit the basket from five feet out than ten feet out, a team makes the most of its scoring opportunities if it works the ball to the open man closest to the basket.

That sounds like a simple formula for winning games, and it is. The problem is that most players don't like to use it. They like to shoot the ball every chance they get. They like to check the score sheets to see how they did after every game. That's fine if all you want to do is score points; but if you want to be a winner, you've got to do everything you can do to help your team. Believe me, it's more fun to score fifteen points in a game that you win than score thirty in a game that you lose.

But before you can even start to think about getting the ball where it needs to be, when it needs to be, you're going to have to learn to throw all the different kinds of passes.

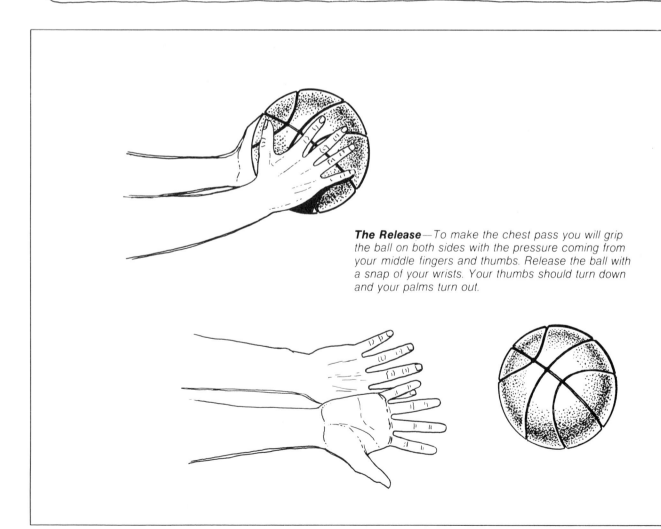

The Release—To make the chest pass you will grip the ball on both sides with the pressure coming from your middle fingers and thumbs. Release the ball with a snap of your wrists. Your thumbs should turn down and your palms turn out.

The Chest Pass

The chest pass is the simplest and quickest pass to throw when there is a clear path between you and your target.

To throw this pass, hold the ball chest high, and grip it on each side with the pressure coming from your middle fingers and thumbs. As you release the ball, step in the direction of the pass with whichever foot feels most natural. Release the ball with a snap of your wrists. Your thumbs should turn down and your palms turn out. This quick, direct pass should travel on a line between your chest and the chest of your receiver.

You will use this pass to move the ball around the perimeter of a defense. It can also be used to move the ball quickly up court on the fast break, and can even be used in traffic if delivered quickly and accurately.

I use this pass whenever I can, because it is the best. And the best pass is the one that gets the job done with the least amount of effort.

Photo by Dick Raphael

I take the ball to the hoop, drawing two defenders. I can either shoot or look to pass to an open teammate.

Photo by Dick Raphael

The Bounce Pass—*With defenders all around, a good way to pass the ball is a quick bounce off the floor.*

The Bounce Pass

The bounce pass is made the same way as the chest pass. The difference is that you pass the ball through the outstretched arms and legs of a defender to a spot on the floor. The spot on the floor and trajectory of the ball are selected so the ball will bounce off the floor and hit the receiver at a point between his knees and his waist.

Since you release this pass just like you do the chest pass, the natural backspin on the ball will take the speed off of it when it hits the floor. That means the bounce pass should be easy for your receiver to handle.

Sometimes, though, I don't want the ball to slow down. When a man breaks free and is cutting away from me to the basket, I don't want to take any speed off of it, or I may not get the ball to him when and where he needs it. In this case, I change my release and push my hands over the top of the ball. My hands end up with my thumbs pointing up, my palms pointing in, and my fingers pointing down. This puts more speed on the ball, but it also makes the ball harder to handle. Use this release only when necessary.

Use this pass to move the ball through heavy traffic by bouncing it to the floor beneath outstretched arms or between defenders. Be sure you can complete it though, because it's a slow pass and easy to intercept.

The Overhead Pass

To make this pass, extend the ball over your head and back a little. Release the ball by snapping your wrists forward. Your palms should end up facing the floor as your fingers point to your target.

You will need to snap your wrists hard to deliver this pass, because you will release the ball high, and want to hit your receiver's hands high, too.

Use this pass to feed pivot men and other players in close to the basket.

Photo by Dick Raphael

I start to make a jump pass over the defense. When I release the ball, my fingers will be pointing to my receiver.

The Baseball Pass

This is the long-range pass; the touchdown pass to a receiver breaking fast to the other end of the court.

Start with your feet shoulder width apart, and plant the foot opposite your throwing arm a step ahead of your other foot. Keep both hands on the ball until you're ready to pass. Then, bring the ball back on your throwing hand until it's in position above and behind the shoulder of your passing hand. At the same time you bring your arm forward in an overhead passing motion, push off your back foot. Continue to bring your arm forward, and release the ball with a snap of the wrist just as you fully extend your arm. Also, make sure to follow through with your arm and wrist motion so you put a slight backspin on the ball. The follow through makes the pass easier to handle and carry farther.

I use this pass to get the ball down court quickly to start fast breaks. Since my receiver is moving fast to the basket, I lead him just as if I were throwing a football pass. My baseball pass arcs over the receiver's head and drops down into his hands.

I don't use this pass unless I'm sure I can get it off; because as soon as I bring the ball back behind my head, I'm in an awkward position. I can't even use the pass when I'm in traffic or closely guarded. I've got to have plenty of freedom to get this pass off.

The Lob Pass

Stand as you would to make the chest pass, but extend the ball high over your head with your elbows slightly bent. Your fingers should be spread over the ball so your hands are slightly behind the ball, and your thumbs point to each other and the center of the ball. Release the ball by snapping your wrists forward and pulling your arms downward. Your hands should end up with palms facing down and fingers pointing to your target.

Put this pass just over the receiver's head. If your receiver has broken free of his defender and is heading for the basket, lead him to the hoop and place the ball so he can continue his motion and lay the ball up for a shot.

Photo by Dick Raphael

The Baseball Pass—*I use this pass only if I'm alone in my own end.*

Photo by Dick Raphael

The Lob Pass—*I get under the ball, and arc it high so it drops over the defense to one of our big men.*

The Hook and Jump Passes

These are especially good passes for good shooters to use, because they utilize the same motions as shots of the same name.

Go up just as if you were going to take a hook or jump shot, but pass off to a receiver at the height of your jump. Snap your wrists, and point your fingers to your target.

Make sure you have a target, or the option of shooting the ball when you leave the ground. You don't want to get stuck in mid-air with nothing to do with the ball.

The Bat Pass

Work on this pass only after you have mastered the others. This pass requires excellent vision and good knowledge of the game.

Because this pass is really the redirection of another pass, you must think about throwing it before the ball is in your hands. You must keep your eyes wide open, and see several things happen at the same time before you choose to use this pass.

Let's say you fake your man and cut hard to the basket. A teammate with the ball spots you and throws a pass. You see the ball on its way into your hands; but at the same time, with your good court vision, you see two other things. You see defenders in the area start to sag in on you, because they know you're going to get the ball in good position. They're going to double and triple team you. Also, out of your other eye you see that one of your teammates is wide open right under the basket. The defense has moved up on you and left him open. You need to get the ball to that man right now. But you're cutting too hard to the basket to stop and throw him a pass. It's time for the bat pass.

Keep cutting to the basket, and as soon as your fingertips make contact with the ball, snap your wrists in the passing motion. Send the ball on to your wide-open teammate. You won't really catch the ball. You'll use the speed on the original pass and redirect the ball. Make sure you follow through and end up pointing your fingers at your target.

***Look Away**—I look one way and pass another. You can see my defender is still playing me for a jump shot.*

The Behind the Back Pass

This is another pass that should be used only when no other will work. It comes in handy when you get boxed in by a defender and have no other way to pass the ball.

When you begin this pass, first tempt your defender a little. Carefully put the ball out to him—just enough so he thinks he has a chance to steal it. Make sure, though, you really have the ball protected with your body. As your defender moves toward you, shift your weight to your passing arm side. Swing your hips from right to left, and bring the ball around your body in the cradle of your hand. Release the ball by snapping your wrist. As in most passes, your fingers should end up pointing at your target.

Drills

There are many drills to help you improve your passing. I have listed a few at the end of the chapter. These can help you master the mechanics of passing, just like shooting practice can help you master your shot. But it will be much more difficult for you to become a good passer than a good shooter. The goal is always up there ten feet off the floor. You can practice out on the court by yourself until you can regularly hit that one spot from about anywhere on the floor. But you never know where you're going to throw a pass. It's always a last second decision. And to be effective, it has to be just as accurate as a shot; plus, it needs to hit its receiver at the right time and with a spin on it that makes it easy to handle. Yes, you can master the mechanics of passing on your own, but you're going to need a lot of help from your coach and a lot of game experience before you become a great passer.

The Right Place, The Right Time, The Right Touch

Five seconds left in the game—you have the ball fifteen feet out, but you're double teamed. Out of the corner of your eye you see a teammate cut to the basket. He has a half step on his man. You go up and fire a jump pass which leads him to the basket. The ball hits his hands as he raises them in the lay-in motion to the basket. He follows through, scores; your team wins the game.

Your imaginary game-winning pass had to be on a line between you and a point right at the beginning of your teammate's shot. That's how every scoring pass must be thrown. Passes thrown too late or too early are intercepted or give the receiver a poor shot at the goal. That's why it's best not to pass unless you're sure you can complete it.

I've worked hard and continue to work hard at developing my passing game. I've studied the game, so I can recognize the precise instant my wrists should snap and send the ball on its way. Another thing that has helped my passing game is my good court vision. I always keep my head up and look straight ahead. I don't focus my eyes on one particular area of the court. I let them relax and take in as much of the court as they can. Everything in my field of vision isn't in perfect focus, but all I'm looking for is movement. All I need to detect is if my teammates are headed in one direction or another; at what speed they're moving; and whether their defenders are on their heels or a half-step behind. I don't need to be able to read the name on a player's jersey before I can throw him a pass. Movement, spacing, speed, and direction are all I need to read.

When I look out on the court, I see offensive and defensive players constantly shifting their positions. It's a never ending battle. Offensive men fake, speed up, slow down, attempting to get open for passes. Defenders react by shifting their feet to keep their bodies positioned between their men and the basket, or their men and the ball. When an offensive man does break open, I see him like a light pouring through an open door at the end of a hallway. And in a split second, I make the decision to fire the ball into my receiver's hands before his defender shuts the door, or before other players block the hallway.

The Bat Pass—*As two defenders close-in, I redirect a pass meant for me to Kevin McHale.*

Photo by Dick Raphael

PASS FIRST, ASK QUESTIONS LATER

My eyes are always peeled for those open doors and hallways. I need to see a safe, open path and a defensive man just enough out of position, before I can let go of a pass. My coaches call these paths a ball can take to a receiver, passing lanes. See the diagram below for some examples of passing lanes.

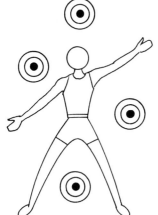

A defender will attempt to keep the passing lanes around him blocked. He will stand in the "ready" position so he can quickly move his hands or body to block whichever lane or target you choose. Always fake a pass to one target before attempting to hit another; or, look at one target and use your peripheral vision to pass to another.

Watch for the target your teammate makes with his hand. He's telling you to hit the bulls' eye. He has positioned his body between his defender and the ball, and can keep the passing lane open.

Your teammates will fake one way and cut another in an effort to lose their defenders. Learn your teammates' moves so you can anticipate and pass the ball where they need it.

When you see a teammate cut to the basket with his defender trailing, lead him to the basket. Hit a chest high target a few feet in front of him.

⊙ Target represents passing lane.

Defenders will sometimes "front" offensive men positioned close to the basket. You can hit your teammate by throwing a lob pass that drops right over his head.

My goal is to get all my passes to the right place, at the right time. But there's one more thing I add to each pass before I call it complete. It's something special. It's something hard to describe. It's like the spin a pool player puts on a cue ball. In basketball it's called "touch." It means that even though I fire the ball to get it to a receiver on time, it's still easy to handle. Because I put a slight back spin on my passes with my follow through, or send the ball with no spin at all my passes are easy for a receiver's hands to meet and control. There are other spins I put on the ball, too. One allows me to shoot a bounce pass quickly to a receiver cutting away from me to the basket. The opposite of that spin will slow a bounce pass so it softly pops up into the hands of a receiver cutting toward me. Those two spins give each pass a different "touch," but ball spin isn't the only element to consider. The weight of force behind the ball also makes a difference in how easy a pass is to handle. I can throw a very quick pass without putting a lot of force behind it. The ball hits my receiver's hands without being too "hot" to handle.

I don't have any diagrams for passing "touch"; nothing to show you how to spin the ball this way or that, or a picture to show you how to throw a fast ball that won't knock your receiver down. The ability to put the right "touch" on each pass is one you develop by playing a lot of "ball." But, I want you to know that a good pass is more than a ball delivered to the right place at the right time. It's one also sent with the right spin, and with just the right amount of force behind it. Like the spin a pool player puts on a cue ball, the "touch" on a pass makes all the difference in the world.

A lot of people call me a great passer. Maybe I am. But it's easy to look good when so few basketball players realize the import ance of passing. Most don't understand it's a key to winning basketball games. And those who understand the importance of passing don't realize it is more than the ability to throw the ball quickly and accurately. Passing is an art that takes years of practice to master. Spend the time. Develop your reflexes. Use your creativity. Become a good passer, and you'll be the most valued player on your team.

Pro Passing Tips

Be sure of your passes—Be sure you can complete a pass before you throw it. You won't gain anything if you throw the ball away.

Look away from your pass—Look away from the direction in which you pass the ball. This will keep the defense guessing your next move.

Pass, then move—Pass the ball, then cut to the basket and look for a pass; work for rebound position; or set a pick. Do something.

Fake before you pass—Make a ball fake before you pass the ball. If you learn this habit, your passes won't be intercepted.

Use the quick release—Snap your wrists and send the ball quickly when you decide to pass. Passing is an all or nothing decision, so send the ball quickly.

Hit your receiver chest high when he's cutting for the basket—Put the ball at chest level so it is easy for him to take it up for a shot.

Receiving a Pass

The pass receiver is on the most important end of the pass. That's why it's important that a player be equally skilled in making and receiving passes.

Every second I'm on the court, I'm alert and ready to receive a pass. When I do see a pass on its way, the first thing I do is relax. I also keep my knees bent, and hold my hands chest high and a few inches away from my body.

I move toward the ball and watch it until it hits my hands. My hands give a little when I receive it.

Photo by Dick Raphael

The Receiver—On the run, I watch a pass all the way into my hands.

33

Practice

1. Alone, stand five or six feet away from a solid wall and pass the ball; direct your pass at a spot on the wall. You can practice all your passes this way, but make sure you concentrate on a particular spot on the wall each time you make a pass.

Also, see how many passes you can make in a minute. See if you can increase the number each day.

This drill will increase your wrist strength, help you learn to concentrate, and help you develop the correct motion for each pass.

2. With another player, play catch, but with two balls. Keep the passes moving back and forth between you as fast as you can without losing control. You will have to alternate chest passes with bounce passes and lob passes to keep the balls from colliding.

This drill will help you learn the passing motions and help you develop your peripheral vision.

3. With two or three players, practice passing on the run. Spread out on the court, and run the length of the floor passing the ball back and forth without letting it hit the floor. At the end of the floor, the player who receives the last pass should lay the ball up for a shot. One player should grab the rebound, and the group should run the drill back the other direction.

Repeat this drill ten times. It will not only help you learn to pass on the run, but will also improve your physical condition and coordination.

4. Another good way to practice passing is to play a game. But before you start, let enough air out of the ball so it is difficult to dribble. This will force everyone to concentrate on passing the ball to get it in shooting position.

Inbound Pass—*This is the toughest pass to make because it must be made within five seconds or the offensive team loses possession of the ball. Also, since every defensive player focuses his attention on the inbound pass, it must be thrown carefully.*

Spectacular Passing—*As far as I'm concerned, makin a great pass is one of the great thrills in basketball.*

SHARPSHOOTING

Ben Rose/Sports Illustrated

"I remember we used to practice in the gym in high school; then, on the way home, we'd stop and play on the playgrounds until eight o'clock. I played when I was cold and my body was aching and I was so tired...and don't know why, I just kept playing and playing.........."

Larry Bird

Like the Wild West gunslingers of an earlier day—free-wheeling, high scoring ball players generate a special excitement, because in basketball the shot is the thrill, the all or nothing, hit or miss quick draw. It's the promise of two points with half a chance to score. And that's close enough to make shooting the ball blood kin to winning. So naturally, as in most sports, basketball glory goes to the scorers, the sharp shooters. But instead of notches in a gun handle, points in a box score track their reputation.

The great ones start just like everyone else. As a kid, in a backyard or on a playground, the shooter begins heaving the orange-brown ball at the hoop six feet over his head. It's tough at first. The ball is a large, awkward pumpkin. His hands are size four. Grabbing the ball is something he does by making a circle with his arms. Hands and forearms clutch the ball to his chest. His chin clamps down for good measure. But the ball likes to bound off the hands, the arms, the chest, maybe the chin, and escape to bounce, and roll about the court as it pleases. The too small hands and too short legs spend a lot of energy corraling the bounding cowhide long enough to sent it in the direction of the goal. The effort's worth it, though, if a few desperate heaves sail through the net. It's a kind of reward to feel the rough leather ball launch off the fingertips, see it silently arch over the rim, and hear it swish as ball rips nylon net.

The challenge of the hoop ten feet in the air, the simple fun that is sinking a shot; these draw millions of players to basketball. But the pull is stronger on some than others. One finds throwing the ball at the hoop an enjoyable way to spend a few childhood hours. He's tickled to see a few shots fall. Another becomes possessed by the challenge of the hoop. The goal is always out there, calling him away from his friends, home, and hot supper to come sacrifice his hours and master the art that is sinking a shot. He does. The shots begin to fall. But no matter how good he gets, he never seems to be satisfied. He just keeps putting them up.

Great shooters start with the rest and end up in a different league. But it's not because they were born with some kind of special talent. And it's certainly not because they were physically stronger. Just a snap of the wrist will send the ball on its way. The great shooters became so because of an attitude they carried around in their heads. They believed that they could master shooting if they worked at it hard enough and long enough. And because of that thinking, they spent the time it took to coordinate a bead on the basket with the hundreds of rhythmic muscle contractions it takes to launch a shot.

Foot muscles arch and create power—muscle power that is transferred up through the body in a ripple of more contractions until it is released by the precisely measured snap of a wrist. That is the shot. But the body must team with the eye before the shot puts the nine inch diameter ball through the eighteen inch diameter rim. They must work together with machine-like precision. And only hours of practice will oil the body-eye machine so it smoothly launches the shot and consistently drops the ball into the gaping mouth over the lip of the rim.

Four or five hours a day, seven days a week, some fifty weeks a year, Pete Maravich sharpened his shooting eye on YMCA and backyard hoops around Clemson, South Carolina. Larry Bird logged similar hours on a playground in French Lick, Indiana. Pete became the NCAA's leading scorer while at LSU; Larry became its fifth leading scorer while at ISU. They both became great shooters because they carried a winner's attitude. They knew if they spent their time and sweat they could be the best. And all their childhood hours did bring them greatness. But even when their achievements put them shoulder to shoulder with the giants in the sport, neither one was satisfied. They kept thinking that if they would work at it a little harder, they could be a little better.

Like Pete Maravich, Larry Bird put on many dazzling performances for home town college fans. When he "cooked," his fans feasted on *haute cuisine*. And they would savor one of his superb shooting-passing-rebounding dishes until he served up another one in the next game. But after many of his stupendous home game performances, while his fans buzzed over his shooting and passing while eating pizza, he would be heading across town, trading one gym for another. He'd trade the 10,000 seat Hulman Civic Center for the thirty seat Boy's Club gym. Only an hour earlier, he had convinced a whole town and visiting team that he was one of the greatest shooters in the game, but he was unimpressed. He thought that if he just practiced a little more he could be better. So he'd be there in the cracker box gym, putting up jumpers and free throws until one or two in the morning.

Great shooters like Larry Bird and Pete Maravich make the decision to dedicate their hours to the pursuit of shooting excellence. There are only rare moments in a game or a season when the sharpshooters really feel they have reached their goal. But it's their tireless grabbing for it that makes them masters of their craft. But once a shooter develops his skills, he has another big decision to make. He has to decide how to use his hard earned talent.

A basketball team needs good shooters like a band needs talented musicians. Sure, a coach can round up any five players, drill them in the fundamentals, put them on the floor, and call them a team. But without players who can make music with the strings of the net, his team won't win. Teams must be able to score to win. Teams must have good shooters to score. But here is where there can be a problem, because good shooters aren't necessarily good scorers.

A team must make the most of every scoring opportunity. It's simple to understand that if two teams shoot fifty shots at the hoop, the team that sends the ball through the hoop the most times wins. It would appear that a team would take the best advantage of its scoring opportunities if it let its best shooter take every shot. That's true, but not in the way it sounds.

The best shooters in basketball hit five or six of every ten shots they take. But they only hit with that kind of accuracy because they carefully select the shots they take. They only put the ball up when they are open for shots in their shooting range and for shots from particular areas of the floor. They know they can hit better from some areas than others, so these are the areas from which they shoot. They are smart shooters. They not only realize their limits and potentials, but also realize that their teammates have their own limits and potentials. This means that the best shooter on the team is the player who on a particular offensive play, has the open shot in good shooting position.

Shooters like to put the ball up every time they can. They think they can win games with their individual shooting talents. They can't. They always find out that a team working in harmony to get the ball to the player in good shooting position beats a one man team. But scorers already know that. It's hard to say how history will look back

The Classic Jumper—Balance, concentration, and touch are the keys to shooting success.

Steve Cadrain Photo

on two of basketball's greatest shooters. But, if in fifty years, you travel to Springfield, Massachusetts and visit the Basketball Hall of Fame, you might find them there back to back on opposite sides of the same tarnished commemorative coin. And there on the side of the display case that houses the coin you might find a button you can push to activate a recorded message. The scratchy recorded voice would probably tell you how "Pistol Pete" Maravich turned the basketball world upside down with his amazing talents and became known as basketball's unrivaled one man band. It might then say that Larry Bird turned it right side up again with his many skills and became known as basketball's most complete team player. While "Pistol" fired at will, Larry fired when necessary, especially when the game was on the line. The tape might go on to say that Pete's one man show was interesting and entertaining for a while, but because his teams rarely won, his tunes began to sound hollow and cheap. On the other hand the message would tell you Larry's orchestral performances were classics, and because his teams usually won, the music he made was deep and rich. The message would end there, but as you're leaving you might glance down at the inscriptions on both sides of the shooter's commemorative coin. One side might say Pete Maravich, Sharpshooter, the other Larry Bird Smartshooter.

UPI/Pam Price

Reverse—*The reverse layup allows me to protect my shot from defenders by positioning the rim and net between their outstretched arms and the ball.*

Photo by Dick Raphael

Going Up—*I concentrate on a spot on the backboard as I go in for the lay-up. I jump up as high as I can, and extend my hand up as high as I can before I release the ball by rolling it off my fingers.*

Photo by Dick Raphael

This is a Percentage Shot?—*Even when I take what looks like an off-balance shot, my body is balanced and I concentrate on my target.*

Photo by Dick Raphael

In Close—*When I get the ball inside, I go straight up with it. I don't stop to dribble. I go up strong, but release the ball with a soft touch.*

Shots through the basket score points. Points light up the scoreboard and tell which team wins. That's why shooting is important to basketball. But it's not really enough for you to become a good shooter. You must become a good scorer if you want to help your team win.

The difference between a shooter and a scorer is this: a shooter puts the ball up every time he has an open shot; a scorer puts it up only when he has the best shot. That doesn't sound like much of a difference, but it's enough of one to mean the difference between winning and losing.

To become a good shooter, you must do three things. First, you must practice and develop your shooting skills. Second, you must learn what shots are good shots for you. Third, you must learn when to shoot.

When I was a kid, I practiced playing "ball," mainly my shooting, four or more hours a day. I practiced shooting with both hands. I practiced all the different shots. I put fakes together with my shots. I worked hard at it, and pretty soon I could hit from all over the court. I was confident of my shot. So when I became a member of a school team, I thought I had it made. But I found out real fast that I had to learn a lot more about shooting if I wanted to help my team win. I had to learn what shots to take and when to take them.

Every player has his favorite shots. I like to shoot from the deep corners or from a spot just to the right or left of the top of the key. Probably because these are the shots I practiced most when I was a kid. You will have your favorite shots, too. So when you're in a game, those are the shots for which you should work. Fake, move without the ball, and get open in your favorite areas of the court, so your teammates can pass you the ball. Remember, the idea is to make every scoring opportunity count. Concentrate on shooting the shots you hit best. Work on your other shots in practice.

But even though you get the ball in one of your favorite shooting positions and are open for a shot, it still might not be the right time for you to shoot. For example, if you spot a teammate closer to the basket than you with an open shot, you should pass the ball to him. I'm sure you have been wide-open under the basket when one of your teammates launched a twenty footer that bounced off the rim. You probably felt like you had been cheated. You had, and your team had, because you both missed the chance for a sure shot at the basket.

There are times, though, when you shouldn't shoot even when you have the best shot. One of those times is when the clock is running out and your team is ahead. At that time, the only shot you should take is a lay-up. Another time you should be careful about putting up a shot is when your team needs a key basket to tie the game or move into the lead with a few seconds left in the game. Be confident you have a sure shot before you put it up.

One time you shouldn't hesitate to shoot is when you've gone cold. When you have one of those games when your shots won't fall, you can't stop shooting. When you're open for the best shot, shoot. It's the only way you can get your touch back. When you're not hitting, though, you should concentrate more on passing to, picking for, and rebounding for your teammates.

The more you play, the more you work and think about shooting and scoring, the better you will be able to use your shooting skills to help your team win. Be more than a shooter. Be a scorer.

Steve Cadrain Photo

Photo by Dick Raphael

Photo by Dick Raphael

The Shot

The jump shot, set shot, lay-up, and hook shot provide you with four different ways to shoot the ball at the basket. But even though each shot will require you to learn a different body and arm motion, you will follow the same sequence of steps to launch each shot. For each shot:

1. Get Ready—Whenever you receive a pass or pick the ball up off the dribble, be sure to grab it so you're ready to shoot. The fingers of your shooting hand should be straight up and spread comfortably on the ball. This means there should be a slight space between the palm of your hand and the ball.

2. Get Set—Whether you're flying through the air shooting a lay-up, or firmly planted on the ground taking the set shot, your body must be balanced. You must have a solid platform from which to begin your shot motion, because an accurate shot is the result of a smooth, rhythmic body and arm motion.

To build this solid platform, stand with your legs spread apart the width of your shoulders. For most shots, the foot of your shooting hand should be shifted slightly ahead of the other. Your head should be straight and on a line that runs through a point in the middle of your stance. Your knees should be slightly bent and your weight concentrated on the balls of your feet.

The farther you are from the basket, the more you'll want to flex your knees, because the power for your shot comes from your feet and legs. Try standing stiff legged, and shoot the ball from about ten or twelve feet. You will feel like you're pushing the ball at the basket. Next, try bending your knees and flexing them at the same time you snap your wrists to release the ball. Notice

how much smoother and easier your shot motion is. Because the power for your shot came up through your legs, your arms and wrists had little work to Do. Their action was used to control the flight of the ball. That's the way it should be.

With your body in balance you can be confident of your shot. And you can always be in balance, even when you're flying through the air, if you keep your head straight, and begin your move to the basket with your knees bent and your weight concentrated on the balls of your feet. Even if you jump in the air, you will have a solid platform from which to shoot if your body is balanced.

3. Aim—When you turn your eyes to the basket, zero in on a spot in the middle of the rim toward the back of the basket. Visualize your target and concentrate on it.

You may choose a different target on which to concentrate, but I use a target in the middle and toward the back of the rim, because:

- If the ball hits the back edge of the rim, the backspin on the ball will force the ball down into the basket.
- If a shot falls short, there are nine more inches of basket into which the ball can fall.
- If a shot is long, there is a good chance it will bounce off the backboard and into the basket.

Another target you can aim at when you're within ten to fifteen feet of the basket is the backboard. When you're shooting from the sides, or running hard at the basket on the fast break, the backboard is a good target. Of course, the target area you choose on the ten square foot board will be different for each spot on the court. This means bank shots require a great deal of

Photo by Dick Raphael

Photo by Dick Raphael

practice, but the time spent learning the target areas of the board will be worth it, because:

- When a shot banks off the board, the ball drops down and has the entire basket to fall into.

- If a shot is fired a little hard off the board, it will still bank in if it hits the right target. That is why I often use the backboard from straight out when I come downcourt on the fast break. Because, sometimes, when I charge hard to the basket, even though I stop quickly to go up for my shot, some of my momentum carries through to my shot. The backboard will control a hard shot and knock it in the basket.

- The backboard is always the best target to use when you shoot a lay-up. It gives you an easy spot to hit when you're charging hard to the basket.

4. Fire—At the peak of your jump or shot motion, quickly release the ball by smoothly moving your arm toward the basket, and snapping your wrists. Release the ball off your fingertips so you give the ball a slow reverse spin.

Also, when you release the ball, send it so it follows an arc-like path of about forty-five degrees. You may want to experiment with higher arcs later, but this one will give good results, and is easy to control. The idea of a high arcing shot is to get the ball high enough over the rim so it can drop straight down into the basket. This gives the ball the maximum eighteen inch diameter of the basket into which the ball can fall.

5. Follow Through—After you shoot the ball, your arm and hand should continue their motion to the basket so your fingers end up pointing at your target. This "follow through" action puts the right spin on the ball so your shots will either hang on the rim or spin down into the basket. The "follow through" action will also make your shot carry a little farther.

6. Follow Your Shot—Follow through and watch your shot all the way to its target, but as soon as your shot hits the goal, be ready to go after a missed shot. This is a difficult habit to learn, because good shooters think all your shots are going in the basket. You, better than anybody else on the court, will have a feel for where the ball will bounce. Go after your shots, because a rebound of your own missed shot usually sets you up with an open shot close to the basket.

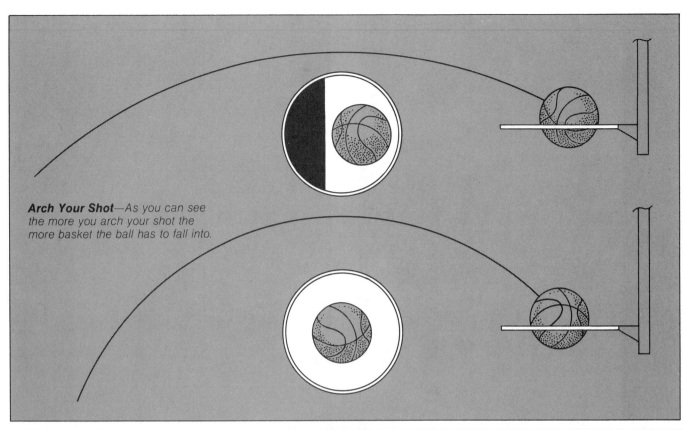

Arch Your Shot—As you can see the more you arch your shot the more basket the ball has to fall into.

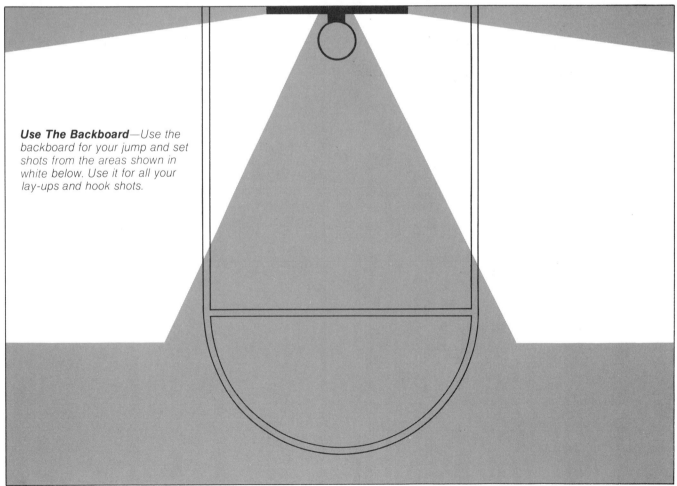

Use The Backboard—Use the backboard for your jump and set shots from the areas shown in white below. Use it for all your lay-ups and hook shots.

Going for Three—*The instant I know I have drawn a foul, I make every effort to put any kind of shot up for a three-point play.*

Photo by Dick Raphael

RK Hubbard

RK Hubbard

The Shots

Now that you understand the basic elements common to all shots, you need to learn the body and arm motions unique to each of the different shots. And it is important for you to learn to shoot the different shots with equal skill. They each have a special advantage; and the ability to shoot a variety of shots will make you an offensive threat from any spot on the court, under any kind of defensive pressure.

The Lay-up

The lay-up is the shot you will use to put the ball up to the basket at the end of a fast break, or any time you drive past your defender and charge down an open lane to the basket. Of course, this is also the shot most teams use to warm up before the start of a game. It gives the players a feel for taking the ball to the hoop with a smooth, unbroken rhythm.

It is important that a player be comfortable moving to the basket with the ball, so your shooting should begin with the lay-up. To shoot the lay-up you will:

1. Get Ready—Dribble toward the basket as fast as you can without losing control of the ball. Also maintain your body balance by keeping your head straight and on a line that runs through the middle of your stance. Your knees will be naturally flexed in the running motion.

If you have trouble moving to the basket with the ball without breaking stride, practice moving to the basket with the same motion, but without the ball. When you feel comfortable doing that, take the ball in your hands and make the same move to the basket, but don't dribble the ball, just stride with it to the basket, and shoot the ball. When you're comfortable with that, try dribbling in and shooting the lay-up.

2. Get Set—As you approach the basket, take-off with your inside foot (foot toward the basket). Push off the floor close enough to the basket so you jump up and not out to the basket. At the same time you push off your inside foot, bend the knee of your outside leg up toward the basket so it is at a ninety degree angle with your body. It will help you stay balanced.

3. Aim—As you carry the ball up to the basket, you should concentrate on a target that is about a foot over the basket, and two to four inches off center, toward your side of the basket. At the top of your jump, your concentration on that spot on the backboard should peak. Don't be distracted. Keep your eye on your target until you see the ball hit your target.

RK Hubbard

RK Hubbard

4. Fire—As you jump to the basket, carry the ball up with both hands until it is in front of the shoulder of your shooting hand. From there, extend your shooting hand to the basket so that your palm faces the basket, and your thumb sticks straight out. As your shooting hand extends to the basket, drop your other hand from the ball to your side to help you maintain your balance.

What I have described above is the forearm delivery of the lay-up. That is, as the ball is being delivered, the back of your hand will face you and you'll roll the ball over your fingers as you release it. This is the best delivery when you are young, and need to put all your power behind the ball to get it to the basket. But it's also a good delivery for any player who wants to power up a shot in heavy traffic.

The underhand delivery is another way for you to shoot the lay-up. When you use the underhand delivery, your hand should be under the ball so that your palm faces straight up to the basket. Release the ball by rolling the ball off your fingers. This is the best delivery to use when you're driving hard to the basket, because it puts the ball softly up on the backboard and gives the ball a spin that pulls it down into the basket.

5. Follow Through—Continue your shot motion so it takes you under the basket.

6. Follow Your Shot—Of all the shots, this is the most difficult one to follow. But, although it puts you in the worst rebounding position on the court, get back into the game as soon as possible. You can come inbounds right under the basket for good offensive rebound position, if the ball stays alive on the rim long enough.

Practice

The lay-up is the highest percentage shot you can take. You should hit every one. But, in a game, you will often take this shot while running full speed at the basket with defenders all around you. That's why you should concentrate every time you shoot this shot.

1. Go to the basket as fast as you can without losing control of the ball, or affecting the accuracy of your shot.

2. Jump up to the basket, and extend your arm to your target.

3. Lay the ball up on the backboard high and soft.

4. Practice shooting your lay-ups with someone guarding you.

5. Practice shooting your lay-ups from both sides of the basket.

The One-Hand Set Shot

The one-hand set shot is the most important shot you will learn. Because, with a few minor alterations, it is the jump shot without the jump, and the free throw without the free throw line. It is also the shot that makes me a triple offensive threat in the NBA.

Most players shoot the jump shot from the field, so defenders play them for the jump shot, or for the drive. When a player guards me, he's got one more thing to worry about. I can shoot the ball as soon as I get it without jumping or dribbling. And since I don't have to jump to shoot the one-hand set, I don't have to commit my intentions to my defender until I release the ball. I can shoot the one-hand set, fake it and drive, or fake it and go up for a jump shot.

The one-hand set shot is the start of your offensive threat, so learn it well. Each time you shoot it:

1. Get Ready—Pick up the ball so you're ready to shoot.

2. Get Set—Relax and balance your body as for any other shot. The foot of your shooting hand should be shifted slightly in front of the other and pointed at the basket.

3. Aim—As you begin to move the ball into shooting position, slightly dip the ball as you flex your knees. Then move the ball into position by pushing it up over, but slightly in front of your head. As you move the ball upward and back toward your shoulder, your elbow will come up and point at the basket, and your arm will fold back as your elbow acts like a hinge.

The foot of your shooting hand should point at the basket. Your elbow, forearm, and hand should all line up with the basket, so you can cock your head a little to one side and use your nose as a sight to line up your forearm with the basket.

4. Fire—Unfold your arm to the basket and snap your wrist forward and downward to put the proper backspin on the ball. As you begin your release, unbend your legs, and raise yourself up on your toes. Remember, the power for all shots comes from your feet and legs.

5. Follow Through—After you release your shot, you should be all the way up on your toes or even slightly off the ground. Your hand should point to your target.

The Triple-Threat Position—From this position I can shoot the one-hand set, fake and drive, or fake and go up for the jumper.

Practice

1. Shoot from the "around the world" positions until you have hit five shots from each position. Then move the semicircle out a few feet and repeat. You can repeat this process until you reach the distance limits of your shooting ability.

2. Another way to practice this shot is to have someone stand in front of you so you have to shoot over their outstretched arms.

3. After you feel comfortable shooting the one-hand set, play a version of one-on-one in which you can only use the one-hand set or the lay-up. Attempt to score on your opponent by either shooting the one hand set over him or by faking it and driving around him.

The Jump Shot

The jump shot is the most widely used shot in basketball. It allows you to jump up and shoot over defenders from any spot on the court. To shoot this shot:

1. Get Ready—While dribbling upcourt, keep your head up, and search for good shooting positions to open. You may see a teammate setting a pick or screen for you, or you may just see that your defender is giving you enough ground that you can move right to one of your favorite shooting positions.

As you dribble to your shooting position, get ready for a jump shot by starting to bend your knees. By the time you reach your spot, your knees should be bent deep enough to give you the power required for your jump.

2. Get Set—When you hit your spot, plant your inside foot (foot toward the basket) and square off with the basket. It is very important that you turn and face the basket squarely before you go up for your shot.

With the foot of your shooting hand pointing at the basket, and your arm, elbow, and hand lined up with your foot, push the ball up into shooting position as you jump straight in the air off the balls of your feet.

Remember, to shoot a smooth, accurate shot, you must have a solid platform from which to shoot. Before you leave the ground you must, balance your body first.

3. Aim—As you leave the ground, zero in on your target. And in the instant before you release your shot, focus all your concentration on that target.

4. Fire—At the top of your jump, unfold your arm to the basket, and snap your wrist forward and downward to give the ball its backspin.

5. Follow Through.

6. Follow Your Shot.

Practice

1. Use the same drills you did for the one-hand set shot.

2. Draw several circles on the court two feet in diameter. Practice dribbling to those spots and shooting your jump shots inside the circle. This will get you in the habit of going straight up and coming straight down.

Photo by Dick Raphael

Peak Concentration—I focus all my concentration on the basket just before I release the ball at the peak of my jump.

The Free Throw

A free throw is just what the name implies. It's a free shot from fifteen feet that is awarded to you because a foul or other rule infraction has been committed by your opponent. You have ten seconds to shoot the ball. All other players line up along either side of the free throw lane in front of your position on the free throw line.

Between twenty and thirty percent of all points a team scores in a basketball game are made from the free throw line. Many games are decided by hit or missed free throws, so you should work for perfection here. Each time you're awarded a free throw you should:

1. Get Ready—Be relaxed and confident when you go to the line. It will, of course, be much easier to feel that way if you have spent many hours practicing your free throws. But whatever your preparation, establish a routine. Every time you go to the line go through the same steps. First, step up to the line, set your feet, and get in a comfortable position. Relax, then to get the feel of the ball, dribble it a couple of times before you bring the ball up into shooting position. Whatever your routine is, go through it before each free throw. Be patient. Relax. You have ten seconds to shoot.

2. Get Set—You should be balanced, and stand as you would for any one-hand shot. The foot on your shooting hand side should be up close to the free throw line and pointed directly at the basket. All the other elements: your elbow, arm and wrist, should line up with the foot so you sight down your forearm at the basket.

3. Aim—Cock your head slightly to one side and use your nose as a sight to line up your forearm with the basket. Concentrate on your target.

4. Fire—Relax, then "break" your wrists and knees at the same time. As you unhinge your forearm and release the ball with the snap of your wrist, you will move up on your toes toward the basket.

5. Follow Through—Your hand should follow the ball to the basket, and your eyes should follow the ball until it hits its target.

6. Follow Your Shot—As soon as you see the ball hit its target, or sense your shot is going to miss, move and get in rebound position.

Photo by Dick Raphael

Photo by Dick Raphael

Photo by Dick Raphael

Photo by Dick Raphael

Practice

There is only one way to practice free throws, and that is to get behind the free throw line and shoot them. When you do practice, always:

1. Repeat each step of your free throw shooting routine.

2. Concentrate on each shot as if it's the one that will win a world championship game.

3. Set goals for yourself. Shoot forty free throws every night and see how many you can hit. See if you can improve your percentage.

The Hook Shot

The hook Shot is the most difficult of all the shots to master, because you begin your shot motion with your back to the basket. But because your back is to the basket and to your defender, this shot protects the ball from the defender and is almost impossible to block.

The hook will require much practice to master; however, it will provide you with a good shot to use in close to the basket. To shoot the hook shot:

1. Get Ready—Many times you will make moves without the ball, like the V-pattern and fish hook moves, which get you open for passes, but position you with your back to the basket. These are perfect moves to set you up for a hook shot. When you get free and receive a pass, grab the ball so you're ready to shoot.

2. Get Set—To get the ball in shooting position, begin from the relaxed shooter's position with legs spread, but hold the ball in both hands about chest high to protect it.

If you're shooting a right-hand hook, turn and slide your foot so it points at the baseline. As you turn and slide on your left foot, lift the ball up with both hands, but take your left hand off the ball so the ball is lying on the fingers of your right hand. Your right arm should now be fully extended away from your body.

3. Aim—Turn your head, and lift your chin up so you can look at your target (it is always best to use the backboard on this shot when you can). As you turn to look at your target, keep turning on your left foot, and raise your right knee and bring it around so it points at the basket. As you turn to the basket, you should move your shooting arm toward the basket in an arc. Your arm should line up with the basket and your right ear, so that when you shoot, the upper part of your right arm will come up and touch your right ear.

4. Fire—When you have lifted the ball to the top of its arc, shoot the ball by snapping your wrist and rolling your fingers under the ball.

5. Follow Through—Keep moving your shooting arm toward the basket until it touches your right ear. Your right arm should be out in front of you, bent at the elbow, for protection and balance. Even after you release the shot, keep turning to the basket so you end up square with, and facing the basket.

6. Follow Your Shot

Practice

1. Practice shooting the hook from the "around the world" positions as you do the jump and set shots, but stay within a ten foot range. Learn to shoot equally well with both hands. And learn to use the backboard.

The Hook Shot—I follow through after releasing a hook shot.

Photo by Dick Raphael

2. Practice the hook with someone guarding you. Have someone stick a hand up, or even a broom, to get you in the habit of shooting a high arcing shot over defenders.

Pro Shooting Tips

1. Learn to shoot all shots with both hands.

2. Before you shoot the ball, look to see how your teammates are positioned on the court. Look to see that one of them is in rebound position.

3. Don't rush your shot.

4. Don't force your shot. You will either have a good shot or you won't. Take only open shots you are confident of hitting.

5. Learn to adjust your shot. If you see that you are consistently shooting the ball short, exaggerate your follow through. Work on your shot if it's missing the mark.

6. When you receive the ball and have a good open shot, don't dribble the ball; shoot the one-hand set or jump shot. There's no reason to waste time dribbling.

7. Be confident of your shot. You've got to believe you can put every shot in the basket.

8. Practice, practice, practice.

"D" ISN'T FOR DEFENSE

"Larry's always close to his man...even if he doesn't go for a block, he's always close enough to bother the shot or the pass. It's instinctive, to read where people are moving, when they like to receive the ball, where. It has to be something inside you that can be developed, but nobody can make you do the things he does."

Bobby Jones, Philadelphia 76'ers forward

Tear any basketball team apart. Go ahead, start at the top, and tear it to the ground. Gather up all the coach's complicated X and O blueprints, and throw them down in a heap. Grab a crowbar and pry the team's passing game apart. Passing fastens the team together. Once you remove it, the structure will collapse, and you'll be able to pick up the rest of the pieces and stack them where you wish. Be careful, however, with the team's shooting. It's a beautiful but fragile fixture. It pleases the fans; it scores the points. Pack it up, and set it out of the way.

OK, now that the team's superstructure is torn to the ground, brush back the debris, dig down and check the foundation—the defense. Check to see if it's solid. Can every square inch withstand an offensive attack, or are there weak spots? Can it repel scoring threats again and again, or are there signs that it could give way as the game progresses? Can it carry the team through any game, no matter what the circumstances, or might it fail when the pressure is on?

Championship teams are built on concrete defense. Arnold "Red" Auerbach knew that back in 1956 when he constructed his new-look Boston Celtics. At the time, experts cast a doubtful look his way. They spotted what appeared to them an obvious flaw in his new design. But the twinkle in his eyes was undiminished. He had good reason to build his Celtic Club around a lanky, bearded, black man whose delight was blocking shots, whose obsession was playing defense. His genius told him his peers had misplaced the key to winning basketball games. They had lost it in their efforts to mastermind spectacular offensive shows. High-scoring big men in the image of Mikan and Petit were the stars in their eyes. Red, though, was unimpressed by shooting stars. He had the idea in his head to found a team on the concrete, immovable, unchangable element of the game—defense. And, of course, while everyone else looked the other way, he signed one William Fenton Russell to a contract. Defense became the name of the game in Boston. And eleven times in thirteen seasons, the world championship flag was hoisted to the rafters in the ancient Boston Garden.

Team Defense—*the defense works only if every player on the court does his job.*

It has been said that genius is the understanding of things simple. And that makes sense when you stop to consider defense's misunderstood importance in the game of basketball. It's value is neither obvious, nor easy to understand. Offense's is.   The sky hook, the slam dunk, the rainbow—the give-and-go, the pick-and-roll, the fast break—they translate into points on the score board. The other end has its steals and blocked shots. But these are rare. Most defense amounts to a defender positioning himself between his opponent and the basket, or his opponent and the ball. That's hard to translate into points. And it's the reason it takes a great basketball mind to look past the obvious kinship between scoring and winning, and see that defense is at least as important as offense.

The roof, walls, and windows are obviously important parts of a house. So are the floors, ceilings, finishes, and fixtures inside. From the look and feel of a house's materials, most people can judge its quality. Or can they? Not really. Not unless they have the knowledge to look past the obvious features and check the building's foundation. It takes the mind of an architect to understand that no matter how beautifully well-built a house appears to be, it can be no better than its foundation. Its wooden structure must rest on a concrete base, or the stress of gravity will pull the house apart. Without a strong foundation, the floor will sink into the mud; the weight of the roof will shift; the unbalanced roof load will break and pull the wall framing apart; that will cause the roof, walls and ceilings to crack; and with time, the once beautiful designed home will be a heap of debris. The wooden structure of a house is not strong enough to

hold together without a solid base—neither is the offensive structure of a basketball team.

Architects of great basketball teams know the offense can't stand alone. It needs to rest on a solid defense. A weak defense would put too much stress on the offense to score points. And the offense isn't always dependable. In fact, offensive teams sputter and spurt through games like high performance cars burning cheap gasoline. One minute, the machine purrs. Everybody's "hot," and the team scores at better than a point-a-minute clip. The next, it misfires. It coughs and struggles along, and can only manage a handful of points in an entire period. Precise timing and touch are additives high powered passing and shooting teams just can't be without. And when they're missing, and the timing is off a tick, and the players lose the touch, the offense falters.

Championships aren't won without great defense. Offensive skills just prove too fragile. They're here and gone, and back again. Defense, though, comes to play every night. Deep down, gut level determination is the main ingredient there, not something as airy as touch or timing. Speed and quickness help too, but it's the stingy desire to deny the offense that does the job. It did the job for the Celtic Dynasty.

Maintain Position—Bird uses the lateral glide step to keep his body positioned between the "Doctor" (Julius Erving) and the basket.

Don't Give an Inch—The "Doctor" commits to the shot, and Bird moves in on him with hands high and feet set in a wide stance.

"D" ISN'T FOR DEFENSE

A Boston team could be down as many as fifteen or twenty points near the end of a game, but not a fan would leave his seat. When the Celtic offense turned sour, and the opposition began to pull away, the defense turned from tough to downright vicious. It became a police action. The man-to-man roped off the court. No more unmolested shots allowed. They closed down the passing lanes. And pity anyone who tried to run the roadblock Bill Russell and company set up around the basket. The Celtic "D" just chewed up the opponent's offense, and spit it out on the other end. Pilfered passes, vacuumed rebounds, and blocked shots fed their hungry fast break. And that was that. Arnold "Red" Auerbach's amazing defensive machine created offense where there had been none, and won, and won, and won.........

The Celtics still win, and win, and win. They still play rugged defense. And Mr. Auerbach is still around, somewhere. But you have to wonder. When you now see another great Celtic, Larry Bird, leave the ground at full speed and dive for a loose ball, you have to wonder what their secret is. How do the Celtics, year after year, field teams with players who play lumberjack defense? Do their great coaches teach it? Is it a brand of defense inspired by such great team leaders as Russell, Havlicek, Cowens, and now Bird? Is it because of something they call Celtic pride? To an extent, these contribute, but defense is floor burns, bruises, and jammed fingers. It's a skill with no scoreboard. It's hard work and no headlines. There's no good reason for a player to work hard on that end of the court, unless, he wants to win more than anything else. And, perhaps, right there is the force that drives a Boston defensive machine.

Winners win. They do because they're different from the rest. They push themselves past the point of pain and exhaustion. They do whatever needs to be done to to grab victory from a challenger. And they don't really know why. There's just a fire inside that pushes them past the limits of their energy and ability.

Desire, winning, defense—it suddenly becomes clear what grasp the man from Boston had of the elements of basketball greatness. He created the Boston Celtics out of his understanding of what the game was, and his vision of what the game could be. He cut through the skin of the game, and revealed defense as its guts. He then picked through the greatest basketball talent in the world, and chose as his players, a handful of individuals who had great talent, but greater desire. And desire drove his great defensive machines. It still does. And the Celtics and Mr. Auerbach still win.

Make it Tough—*Bird shows he doesn't have to block the shot to be an effective defender. Here he has forced the "Doctor" into an awkward, low percentage shot.*

Jim Cummins Photo

Defense is half the game of basketball. And just as you can't run half a race and expect to be a winner, you can't play on one end of the court and expect to be a champion. A lot of players come into the NBA with great shooting and passing talents. But unless they learn to play great defense, they don't play in this league. And defense is equally important in whatever league you play, that is, if you want to be a winner.

Fundamentally, defense is a simple skill. It amounts to keeping your body positioned between your opponent and the basket. It's about as simple as that. But mentally, defense is tough. You've got to use your mental toughness to constantly push your body around the court so that it says no to your opponent, 'No, I'm not going to give you good shooting position! No, I'm not going to let you drive around me! No, I'm not going to let you pass the ball around me! No, I'm not going to let you slip around me into rebound position! No, I'm not going to let you do what you want to do with the ball.'

Of course, your opponent is going to score on you. He's going to be able to do some things he wants to do with the ball. But that will be the test of your determination. Each time he's successful, get tougher. Talk to yourself. Push yourself, again and again, into positions that say 'no' to your opponent. Don't give him an inch until the final buzzer sounds.

It takes guts to play defense, because you can loaf out on the court and nobody will know it. Only you will know if you did your best to grab a loose ball, or stop your man from scoring. You've got to push yourself to do your best. And when you do, don't expect headlines or pats on the back. Most fans, and many of your teammates won't realize that every point you deny your opponent is just as important as every point you score. But as an intelligent player, know the importance of defense, and realize it's just one of those tough jobs that has to be done if you want to be a winner.

To be able to play good defense, you'll have to practice it about as much as you practice your shooting. That will be hard. Shooting is fun. Defense isn't. But take it from me, it's fun to win games. And you can't win games, you can't become a champion, unless you learn to play good defense.

Going for it—Here I go for a steal, but try to keep from fouling.

Defensive Stance

The first thing you need to realize about your defensive assignment is that your opponent has a slight advantage. He has the ball and knows where he wants to go. You don't. He'll always have a split second head start. That's why you need to be alert and ready to move quickly at all times.

Because you must react with every move your man makes, defense begins with the way you stand on the court. You must be able to respond to a fake or a move without losing your balance. To get in the ready stance, stand with your feet about shoulder width apart. Keep your feet square, or stand with one foot slightly in front of the other in what's called the boxer's stance. The important thing is that your body is balanced between both legs so you can easily move in any direction. Your weight should be evenly distributed over the soles of your feet. If you're in the boxer's position, though, shift a little more weight to your back foot. Whichever stance you use, your stance and even weight distribution will give you a solid platfrom from which to work.

With your body balanced, keep your back straight, and bend your knees so your hips are low. Extend your hands and arms from your body between chest and waist height. Your arms should be slightly bent at the elbows, and your hands should be open and relaxed.

In the ready position, you're balanced and your arms and legs are cocked and ready to fire off in any direction. But you must also concentrate on your man so you can react immediately to his moves. Before your man gets the ball, keep an eye on his chest. It's the only area of his body he can't fake. It goes where he goes. While you keep an eye on him, though, use your peripheral vision to keep track of the ball and the other activity on the court. Be alert to all action on the court until your man gets the ball. When he has it, the pressure is on you. Concentrate on his chest, and now use your peripheral vision to keep track of what he's doing with the ball. You have to be ready not only to keep your body between your man and the basket, but also to block passes or shots he may try to make.

Photo by Dick Raphael

Ready Position—*in this position I am ready to respond to whatever move my opponent might make.*

FANCY FOOTWORK

Basketball isn't at all like football. You don't protect your goal by knocking your opponent to the ground. Basketball defenders are a little more civilized. They defend the basket by blocking an opponents access to it with their bodies. They constantly shift their feet to keep in what's called good defensive position.

You might block a few shots or passes during a game, but 90% of the time your defensive effort will consist of a lot of fancy footwork that keeps your body in a position that discourages the efforts of your opponent. Below you will find illustrations and explanations of the three different steps you'll need to learn to keep your body in the right position at all times.

Lateral Glide Step

Use this step to move from side-to-side. From the ready position, move in the desired direction by lifting both feet at the same time and gliding across the floor. The entire surface of your shoe soles should contact the floor as you land. Pretend you are a crab gliding across the beach. That is the kind of motion you should use to make the lateral glide step.

Approach Step

This step begins from the boxer's stance. Move straight ahead by lifting both feet and gliding as you did to make the lateral glide step. The difference will be that one foot will advance in front of the other. Making your approach with the boxer's stance allows you to move in and distract a man with the hand and arm, but at the same time forces you to keep one foot back in case you need to retreat to the basket.

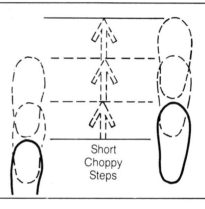

Short Choppy Steps

Retreat Step

This step allows you to give ground to the offensive man without losing your balance or position. It is made the same way as the approach step, but in the opposite direction.

If caught in open court, however, you may find you can't retreat quickly enough to stay between your man and the basket. In this case you will have to shift your weight to the balls of your feet, and run backwards to maintain your position. If you still can't maintain position, you will have to execute the crossover step. This means you cross one leg over the other so you can turn and run straight ahead. Intercept your man before he reaches the basket, and reestablish your position.

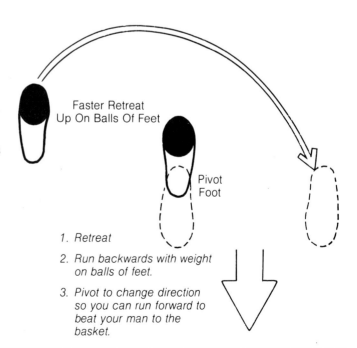

Faster Retreat
Up On Balls Of Feet

Pivot Foot

1. Retreat

2. Run backwards with weight on balls of feet.

3. Pivot to change direction so you can run forward to beat your man to the basket.

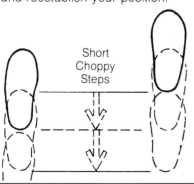

Short Choppy Steps

Defensive Positions To Use
When Opponent Is Without The Ball

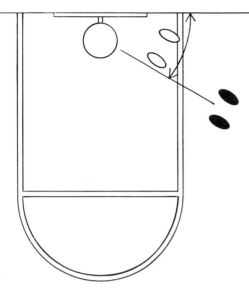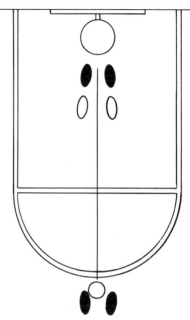

When guarding a man in this position, play him slightly to the baseline. If he gets free toward the middle you should get help from your teammates. If he gets around you on the baseline, though, you're in real trouble.

When your man is in close to the basket you can't afford for him to get the ball. If he gets the ball in close, he'll take the ball up and force you to foul him or give him a good shot. So move around him and "front" him. Get in the ready stance and stay between your man and the passer.

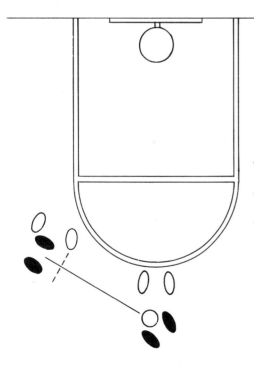

When in this position, focus your attention between your man and the passer. Position yourself so you can stick your hand in the passing lane to discourage the pass. Wedge your man in with your feet as shown, so he can't easily turn and cut to the basket.

Watch and Learn

Each second you're on the defensive end, you must be alert to your man, the ball, and the movement of other players on the court. But it's when your man has the ball that you've got to be at your best. The pressure is on you to keep him from scoring. So turn that pressure around and put it on him. Move in on him, get your hands up, and move them up and down around him. Harrass him. Don't give him a moment's rest.

But at the same time you put on the pressure, remember the split second advantage the offensive man has over you. Be ready for his move. And one of the best ways to be prepared for his moves is to learn more about the way he plays the game. Watch the way he shoots, the way he does his passing. If you learn from what you see, you'll be able to better anticpate his next move.

Here are some examples of things I look for when I guard a man:

- If I see that a player dribbles with the same hand all the time, I overplay him to his favorite side. I force him to use his weak hand.

- If I see a player likes to shoot from particular areas of the court, I try to beat him to his spot. I keep him out of his shooting positions.

- If he makes the same fakes every time downcourt. I note that and play him accordingly.

- If he likes to use the same passing lanes most of the time, I remember that and am ready to bat down his passes.

Offensive Defense

Don't wait for the man with the ball to make the first move. Let him know right away that he's in for the toughest game of his life. Go after him. Take the game to him instead of waiting for him to bring it to you. Take away his split second edge. Make him respond to you. It will ruin his game plan.

Here are some things I do when I play offensive defense:

- I pick my man up as soon as he crosses the ten-second line. There's no reason for me to let him move to within fifteen feet of the basket before I guard him. Besides, it lets him know the pressure is on.

- I jump on jump shooters. I move in on jump shooters until we're shirt-to-shirt. I use a wide stance so if the shooter decides to forget the shot and try and drive around me, he'll have to work at it. Also, when I play this aggressive defense, I expect my teammates to help out if my man does get around me.

- I constantly harrass the man with the ball. I keep my hands moving up and down around him. If I reach for the ball, I also make an approach step with both feet so I don't throw myself off balance. And when I go for the steal, I stick my hand straight in with my palm up. I don't slap at the ball, I just make an upward flicking movement at it.

- I overplay the dribbler. I know that 99% of all dribblers prefer one hand over the other. I overplay on a dribbler's favorite side. If the dribbler prefers the right hand, I line

Double Up—*double teaming the man with the ball is an effective way to force offensive mistakes.*

up my nose with the dribbler's right shoulder. I move ahead of him in his direction of dribble, and force him to switch dribbling hands, or stop his dribble altogether.

- I use head and body fakes just like an offensive man. I keep the offensive man off balance with these fakes, and force him into making moves he doesn't want to make.

Defensive Defense

Even though you can agressively attack the man with the ball, he still has the ball; and although you make it hard on him, he will still be able to shoot, pass, and dribble the ball. When he does, you will need to know how to react to these offensive threats.

When I'm on defense, here are a few of the ways I respond to my opponent when he threatens with the shot, pass, or dribble:

- I keep my hand up about shoulder high in front of my man's shooting hand all the time he is in shooting range.

- I block my man away from the basket as soon as he shoots his shot.

- I keep my eye on my man when he passes the ball. I don't watch the ball, because I would lose track of my man.

- I keep myself between my man and the basket.

- I beat my man to the ball. If my man cuts to the ball from the weak side (the side away from the ball) I beat him to it.

- When my man is on the strong side (the side of the court the ball is on) I overplay him a little and stick my hand in his passing lane. I make him work for the ball.

- I help my teammates when their men beat them. If a man slips past one of my teammates and is on his way to the basket with the ball, I will switch off my man, and establish defensive position on the man with the free lane to the basket.

- I talk on defense. I call out "switch" when I get caught in a pick or screen. I call out "pick or screen" when I see one forming. I call out "shot" when I see an opponent has put the ball up for a shot. I talk to keep teammates informed. A defense works better when it communicates.

Photo by Dick Raphael

Keep Your Guard Up—*I use my position to keep my man from cutting to the ball easily.*

Fouls

How many times does it happen? The clock has all but run out. A team is down one point, but has a man at the line with a one on one. His free throws will win, lose, or tie the game. A foul gave him the chance to do all those things.

Fouls and resulting foul shots decide many games. Most are committed because players are caught by surprise. Either they haven't studied their opponents offensive moves, or they weren't concentrating on the game. But fouls aren't always bad.

If the man we talked about before was at the free throw line because his defender was caught off balance, or not paying attention, the defender's coach would surely be upset. But if he had fouled because his man had slipped through the defense and was headed for a sure two points, the coach would regard his move as a "smart" foul. It would be better, in that case, to make the shooter hit two shots under pressure, than to give him a free shot that would "ice" the game.

There are other special situations in which a foul would be a good defensive move, but except for such special situations, fouls should be avoided. Fouls not only give an opponent free shots at the basket, but can also put you on the bench. By concentrating and playing fundamental defense, you will avoid unnecessary fouls.

Jim Cummins Photo

Foul!—I don't overact, but I sometimes let out a gasp or put a pained expression on my face to help the referee realize I was fouled.

Shot Blocking

Shot blocking is a spectacular defensive play. It's a defender's greatest moment. It's a shooter's worst. Mastery of this skill requires good concentration, balance, timing, and leaping ability. It requires good judgement too, because it's a defensive tool to be used with great care.

Bill Russell was probably the greatest shot blocker in NBA history, yet as great as he was, he only expected to block one or two shots out of every ten a shooter attempted. But he knew he didn't have to block every shot to be effective. He got a lot of mileage out of each block he made. Once he blocked a player's shot, he would make the shooter think. The shooter would start concentrating on how to get the ball over Mr. Russell, instead of on making the shot. It would be just enough to throw off his aim. And about the time he recovered his confidence and shot rhythm, "thawaak," the ball would be in his face again.

One key to shot blocking is knowledge of a shooter's habits. Watch your opponents and pay attention to the rhythm and motion of their shot. Pay attention to the way they bring the ball up into shooting position from the passing or dribbling position. Many times you can knock the ball away as the shooter brings the ball up in front of him to load his shot. But be patient. Don't go looking for a shot to block. Good defense means maintaining good defensive position. Don't swat at the ball and risk a foul, or risk losing your position. But, whenever you see you can block a shot without fouling the shooter, go ahead, put it in his face. Then see how much mileage you can get out of your spectacular defensive play.

When I block a shot:

- I count 1000-1 to myself as I see a man begin his shot motion. If I hesitate one second, I wait long enough to guarantee myself that the shooter is committed to the shot. It is also the right timing to get me to the peak of my jump at about the time the shooter is ready to release the ball.

- I make sure I jump straight up and not into the shooter.

- I concentrate on the ball.

- I block the shot with my right hand when the shooter shoots from the left side of the court, and with my left hand if he shoots from the right.

- I flick at the ball with my fingers. I don't slap at it.

- I try to recover the ball after I've blocked the shot.

Skywalking—*I jump straight up, and flick at the bottom of the ball to cancel Doctor J's (Julius Erving's) house call.*

Practice

The Two Box Drill—Use the lateral glide, the approach, and retreat steps to follow the two box pattern as shown below.

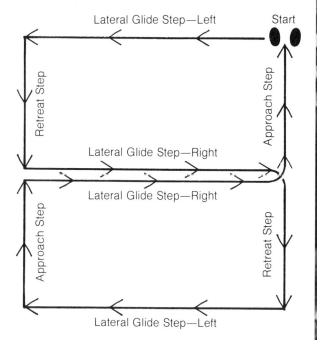

Lateral Glide Step—Left   Start

Retreat Step

Approach Step

Lateral Glide Step—Right

Lateral Glide Step—Right

Approach Step

Retreat Step

Lateral Glide Step—Left

One-on-One—Find one of your friends and go one-on-one the length of the court. One player will get in the ready stance and practice guarding the other player as he dribbles downcourt. Switch positions, and repeat in the opposite direction.

The very best way to practice defense is to play as much one-on-one, two-on-two, or whatever kind of game you can get going. Use the opportunity to concentrate on your defensive skills.

A Little Help—Defense is a team effort. Here Kevin McHale helps me protect the basket.

Photo by Dick Raphael

BASKETBALL

LARRY BIRD

Birthdate: December 7, 1956
Birthplace: French Lick, Indiana
High School: Spring Valley
French Lick, Indiana

College: Indiana State '79
Height: 6 feet, 9 inches
Weight: 220 pounds

An incredible, multi-talented package wrapped in linebacker toughness—a player who performs athletic feats with all the delicate, timely control of a piano concert master—Larry Bird is a basketball dream.

But pinch yourself. He is real. He pounds the boards, charges fearlessly to the hoop, and plays a bruising brand of defense. Yet his true strength isn't his strength. It's his mastery of the game's subtle elements.

Larry Bird's traveling, sleight-of-hand passing show delights fans on the NBA circuit. His well-timed execution of the give-and-go is a phenomenon. His trunk full of mesmerizing ball-and-body fakes leaves defenders grasping at air. They shudder, too, as the Bird glides through their hands. They know he can unleash a devastating ambidextrous arsenal of shots.

What a box of tools the master craftsman of the hardwood brings to work. And Mr. Bird uses his tools, expertly, to do one thing—win. An impressive pile of statistics means nothing to him. He looks for the final verdict in the scoreboard lights. That's why he dives onto the floor for loose balls and takes brutal punishment in return for rebounds and key shots. And it's why he uses his dart-like passing to make his team work. He just flat out wants to do everything humanly, or ''Birdly'' possible to help his team win. That's what Larry Bird is about.

Add one Bird to any other four basketball players, and something extraordinary happens. The combined elements of his amazing individual skills and winning attitude react within the team structure in an unexpected way. He doesn't just improve his team by overwhelming the opposition with his personal stats, he somehow inspires each of his teammates to dig up every ounce of talent they have and put it on the line.

His unique ability to bring out the best in others is unexpected. It's magical. But it's also understandable when you see him in action. He might as well have walked over and gently placed the ball in a teammate's hands, and said, "Here's the ball, there's a wide open shot. Take it. I know you can hit it." That's how you might describe the effectiveness of one of Bird's great passes. They're precious gifts from out of nowhere, products of an unusual generosity that infects whomever walks onto the court with him.

His desire, too, is contagious. Without regard for the burns and bruises, he hurls his body at the game. He melts away every other player's excuse to hold anything back. And when he has spent himself on a game, and hands the credit for victory to his teammates, or accepts for himself the blame for defeat, there is nothing left to say.

Larry Bird is a whopping influence on the game, its players, its fans. No one who sees him perform can help but be moved to stand up and cheer.

LARRY BIRD'S NBA RECORD
Regular Season

Year	G	FGM	FGA	Pct	FTM	FTA	Pct	Reb	Off	Def	Ast	Pts	Avg
79–80	82	693	1463	.474	301	360	.836	852	216	636	370	1745	21.3
80–81	82	719	1503	.478	283	328	.863	895	191	704	451	1741	21.2
81–82	77	711	1414	.503	328	380	.863	837	200	637	447	1761	22.9
82–83	79	747	1481	.504	351	418	.840	870	193	677	458	1867	23.6
83–84	79	758	1542	.492	374	421	.888	796	181	615	520	1908	24.2
84–85	80	918	1760	.522	403	457	.882	796	164	678	531	2295	28.7
85–86	82	796	1606	.496	441	492	.896	805	190	615	557	2115	25.8
86–87	74	786	1497	.525	414	455	.910	682	124	558	566	2076	28.0
87–88	76	881	1672	.527	415	453	.916	703	108	595	467	2275	29.9
TOTALS	711	6991	13938	.502	3310	3713	.891	7236	1567	5715	4367	17783	25.0

Playoff

Year	G	FGM	FGA	Pct	FTM	FTA	Pct	Reb	Off	Def	Ast	Pts	Avg
79–80	9	83	177	.469	22	25	.830	101	22	79	42	192	21.3
80–81	17	147	313	.470	76	85	.894	238	49	189	103	373	21.9
81–82	12	88	206	.427	37	45	.822	150	33	117	68	214	17.8
82–83	6	49	116	.422	24	29	.828	75	20	55	41	123	20.5
83–84	23	229	437	.524	167	190	.879	252	62	190	136	632	27.5
84–85	20	196	425	.461	121	136	.890	182	53	129	115	520	26.0
85–86	18	171	331	.517	101	110	.918	167	49	118	147	466	25.9
86–87	23	216	454	.476	176	193	.912	231	41	190	165	622	27.0
87–88	17	152	338	.450	101	113	.894	150	29	121	115	417	24.5
TOTALS	145	1331	2797	.476	825	926	.891	1546	358	1188	931	3559	24.5

CAREER HIGHLIGHTS

1978–79
- Finished college career 5th leading scorer in NCAA history.
- Consensus All-American and NCAA Player of the Year.
- Led Indiana State University to an undefeated season and to the final game of the NCAA finals.

1979–80
- NBA Rookie of the Year.
- All-NBA First Team.
- Eastern Conference All-Star team.

1980–81
- Celtics won NBA Championship.
- All-NBA First Team.
- Eastern Conference All-Star team starter.

1981–82
- All-NBA First Team.
- Eastern Conference All-Star team starter.
- All-Star Game Most Valuable Player.

1982–83
- All-NBA First Team.
- Eastern Conference All-Star team starter.
- Established career and Celtics' single-game scoring high of 53 points on March 30, 1983, against the Indianapolis Pacers.

1983–84
- Celtics won NBA Championship.
- Set NBA record for most points in the playoffs (632).

- NBA Most Valuable Player.
- NBA Playoffs Most Valuable Player.
- All-NBA First Team.
- Eastern Conference All-Star team starter.

1984–85
- NBA Most Valuable Player.
- All-NBA First Team.
- Eastern Conference All-Star team starter.
- Broke career and Celtics' single-game scoring high with 60 points on March 12, 1985, against the Atlanta Hawks.

1985–86
- Celtics won NBA Championship.
- NBA Most Valuable Player.
- NBA Playoffs Most Valuable Player.
- All-NBA First Team.
- Eastern Conference All-Star team starter.
- Led NBA in free-throw percentage (.896).

1986–87
- All-NBA First Team.
- Eastern Conference All-Star team starter.
- Led NBA in free-throw percentage (.910).

1987–88
- All-NBA First Team.
- Eastern Conference All-Star team starter.
- Averaged 29.9 points per game, his career high.
- Free-throw percentage .916, his career high.

BOUND!!!

"Bird is not a great leaper, but just has a sense of when to go up for a rebound."

Bob Cousy

²re•bound \'rē,baund, ri-'\ *n* 1 a : the action of rebounding : RECOIL b : an upward leap or movement : RECOVERY 2 a : a basketball or hockey puck that rebounds b : the act of taking a basketball rebound 3 : an immediate spontaneous reaction to setback, frustration, or crisis

Webster's Seventh New Collegiate Dictionary

Webster has a skeleton meaning for about every thing or activity on earth. And each rawboned explanation is alphabetically displayed in his word museum. If you look up the word "rebound" you'll find the above definition, but until you look the flesh and blood animal in the eye, you can't know what rebounding is about in the real world of hoops and hardwood.

Webster had the right idea. The basketball is elastic, and will leap up and off the rim when a shot misses the mark. The definition "the act of taking a basketball rebound," however, provides a boney description of what happens when the ball falls into a crowd of hungry players. Snakepit, hole, trench—names given the six foot semicircular area around the basket, connote the true nature of life after missed shots. It's a jungle down there. It's the domain of the big, strong, quick animals, the rebounders. They scrap and claw for every leather morsel that drops off the rim. Pushing, grabbing, elbowing—they're facts of life. It's instinctive of this species to love physical contact. Yet the force that drives them is a natural desire to possess the ball. Rebounders will do anything within the basketball law to capture their prey, and feed their fast break.

Larry Bird is one of the breed. He's not one of the biggest, strongest, or quickest animals in the NBA land of giants, but he is certainly one of the best rebounders anywhere. But it's easy to ignore his rebounding chores. It's a lot more fun to forget the hard work; sit back, and enjoy his wheeling-and-dealing passing show, or take note and appreciate his artistic soft-touch "rainbows." Loose with the ball, he's a virtuoso performer. But tangled in the snake pit, he's reduced to just another hard-working player, sweating, struggling, paying his dues for the ball. It's not a pretty sight. But if the price he pays in the pit reflects the value of a rebound, each one he scrounges is worth two fancy passes, or two artistic shots.

Making Contact—*As soon as Larry knows the ball is on its way to the hoop, he blocks out and makes contact with his man. He maintains that contact so he can keep track of his opponent while he looks for the ball.*

Physical punishment is the price rebounders pay to control the boards. Fans don't notice the pain, three rows up in bleacher seats, but it's there, down on the floor. There is, though, at least one Bird fan who understands the price and the pain. *"We were all sittin around the Bally, talkin about ISU's next NCAA tournament game with Oklahoma. You see, it was Larry's last year of college, and we knew if ISU ever had a chance to go all the way, it was this year. Larry was just standing over there, a few feet from where we arm chair coaches were hashing out our strategies. We started talkin about how rough the game would be cause Oklahoma was very physical. Somebody got up the nerve to shout out, 'Hey Larry, is it as rough as it looks out there. Isn't basketball supposed to be a non-contact game.' We all laughed a little. Larry gave a little smile. And we waited for him to say something. But he just walked over, and right in front of everybody pulled up his shirt. He showed us some of the ugliest plum-purple bruises we'd ever seen. They was all over his body about elbow high. Everybody got a little quiet for a spell."*

Whatever the punishment, the great players take it. Because it's rebounds that put the offense to work. Depending on who you talk to, possession of the ball is worth one or one-and-one-half points to a team's offense. That's all theoretical stuff, of course, but when a coach puts that together with the fact that about ninety-five free balls ricochet off the rims in a typical 100 point game, he becomes very interested in recruiting rebounders. In his imagination he can see his star player pulling down fifteen rebounds, and then the scoreboard lighting up not fifteen, but thirty points. Thirty, because he figures fifteen for possession, and figures another fifteen for the points the opposition lost each time his team took the ball away.

Larry Bird doesn't go in for all that theoretical jazz. He doesn't take a calculator out on the court and figure the odds of rebounds turning into points. He just walks on the court and does his job. It's instinctive. It's a part of his aggressive nature to want the ball—all the time. And he goes after it with all his energy, because he doesn't have to make any calculations to know his team can't win unless it controls the boards. It's easy to understand that rebounds feed the offense and keep it working at the job it does best. But to keep the offense working to score points, Larry has to spend most of his energy "pogoing" for the ball with two-hundred-and-fifty pound opponents hanging on him.

The brute strength and calculated quickness of a wrestler help the good rebounders gain and hold rebounding position. And leaping ability helps, even though 75% of all rebounds are taken below the rim. But the attribute that allows Larry Bird to be a leading rebounder in the NBA, is his uncanny ability to look out the corner of his senses, and feel-see the ball on its way to the hoop a quarter second before anyone else. He has the center fielder's sixth sense. He anticipates the crack of the bat and is moving into position before ball leaves bat. You don't see him do it. He's just there when the ball comes down. Chalk up another "bound."

Photo by Dick Raphael

Explode For The Ball—Larry blasts off the floor and grabs the ball at the peak of his jump. Notice, too, that his body is positioned between the ball and his opponent.

Bound!! Get on the boards and grab every rebound you can get your hands on. Your team needs the ball to score. But a rebound doesn't just give your team a chance to score, it defuses your opponent's offensive threat. Possession of the ball is everything to an offense. That's why teams that control the boards, win games.

You will find rebounding to be the roughest job you do on the basketball court. It requires a lot of strength and quickness to compete for the ball. Many times, eight or more hands will be grabbing for the ball at the same time. Every other player will want the ball for the same reason you do. The secret is to want it more. And that doesn't mean you think about getting the ball more than other players. It means you practice rebounding fundamentals more than other players. It means you train harder so you are stronger and in better shape than your opponents. It means you study the game, and learn to anticipate, and judge the way rebounds come off the rim. It means that if an opponent goes up for the rebound five times, you go up six.

Rebounds = shots = points = games won—a simple equation, but one that won't compute if you don't supply the rebounds. The only way you're going to get them is to set your mind to it. Don't ever quit going for the ball. There's no excuse for it. Anyone can quit. Going after rebounds is like reaching for goals you set for yourself. You'll never reach them unless you keep trying. Never give up!

Defensive Rebounding

If the first rule of defense is to keep between your man and the basket, the second is to block out your man as soon as you see an opponent shoot the ball. The "blocking out" prevents the offensive man from getting in a position from which he can tip-in the ball, or get a rebound and shoot the follow-up shot.

The team theory of defensive rebounding is based on the formation of a protective triangle around the basket. One player positions himself in the middle of the foul lane, while two others stand on either side of the basket near the lane markers. When the ball goes up, all three pivot and face the basket. They position their bodies so they fence off a triangular area around the rim. The ball can bounce into their area and be grabbed without interference from an offensive player.

Before a team's rebounding works, however, each player must be able to secure his position, and keep himself positioned between his man and the basket when he turns to go for a rebound. Here are some important things to remember about defensive rebounding:

1. Anticipate the shot. You not only need to keep an eye on your man at all times, but you also need to stay alert to the movement of the ball and other players on the court. Look for action that signals a shot is being taken, or probably will be taken. For instance, if you see a guard cut off a pick, you can generally expect him to take the shot or drive to the basket for a lay-up. Split your vision when you spot this kind of activity, and as soon as you see the player is committed to the shot, move into rebounding position. Anticipate the shot, but don't turn for the rebound until the ball is in the air; because your first duty is to protect the goal from your man's offensive threat. If you turn too soon, the man with the ball could easily pass the ball off to your man, and he would have an easy shot.

Photo by Dick Raphael

***Blocking Out**—After I make contact, I set my feet in a wide stance, and wall off an opponent's path to the ball.*

2. Block out and establish your position. If you are playing good defense, you will be positioned between your man and the basket when the shot goes up. In order to turn for a rebound and keep your man blocked out, you must use the forward or reverse pivot. Use the pivot and block out your man as follows:

- Use the reverse pivot when you are within the free throw area of the court. You should already be facing your man and be in the boxer's stance. Make a crossover step with your right foot, and plant your right foot in front of or just to the right of your opponent's right foot. Pivot around on your right foot, so you face the basket, and shield your man from the goal with your body.

ward for the ball. If you have to go straight up for a ball, your opponent will have just as good a chance to grab the ball as you do.

4. Locate the ball as soon as possible. As soon as you pivot around, start looking for the ball. The trajectory and area from which the ball was shot can tell you where the ball might rebound.

5. Explode off your toes for the ball. Be patient, but as soon as you see the ball is within your reach, blast up after it so you grab it at the peak of your jump.

6. Grab the ball. Don't tip or bat the ball on your defensive board. Get hold of it and protect your goal.

Before a shot goes up, you should be in good defensive position between your man and the basket.

As soon as you anticipate the shot, reverse pivot. Place your right foot in front of your opponent's right foot, plant your right foot and pivot around so you face the basket. As you pivot, assume a semi-crouched position and use a couple of short, backward steps to ram your buttocks into the upper portion of your opponent's legs. Remember to stick your arms out so you are as big as you can be. Maintain contact while you locate the ball.

You should keep your opponent as far away from the basket as possible so you can jump forward for the ball.

- As soon as you pivot around, assume a semi-crouch position. Stand with your feet in a wide stance. Lift your arms and stick your elbows out. The idea is to keep your man away from the ball, so make yourself as big as you can by sticking out your arms and assuming a wide stance.

- As soon as you pivot and block your man out, make contact with your opponent. This is important, because it lets you keep track of him while you turn your vision and attention to the bounding ball. Use short backward steps to ram your buttocks into the upper leg areas of your man. Maintain this contact until you go for the ball.

3. Establish your position so you keep your man as far away from the basket as possible. That way there is an area for the ball to fall into, and you can jump for-

7. Protect the ball. Grab the ball, come down with it, and snap the ball into your body so that your elbows stick out. Then give the ball a half spin so one of your hands is over the top of the ball, and the other is underneath it. Pivot, and make the outlet pass. As soon as you have the ball secured, you become an offensive player. Carefully pivot around and face your goal. Use your good court vision to pick up one of your teammates cutting down court. Get the ball as far down court as you can. Your rebound is the starting point of the fast break.

Be careful when you make the outlet pass, because the man you had been blocking out is now a defensive man. And if he is a good defender, he will wait for you to pivot around, and try to steal the ball. It is important to get the ball downcourt quickly after the rebound is taken, but throwing the ball away on your opponent's end of the court is the worst thing you can do. Be careful.

Offensive Rebounding

The basket is an apple tree. Rebounds are its apples. Your defensive man is a fence around the tree. You want the apples, but you either have to wait for them to fall on your side of the fence, or carefully jump up and grab for them without hurting yourself on the fence. The only other way you can pick the apples is to find a hole in the fence somewhere and squeeze through, but that's hard to do.

That's the story of offensive rebounding. It isn't easy, and there's no way to make it that way. Defensive rebounding is tough enough, but an offensive rebounder starts with a man between himself and the basket. He has to want the ball twice as much as his opponent to have a shot at it.

If an offensive rebounder can position himself between his man and the basket, he uses the very same rebounding fundamentals we discussed for defensive rebounding. When I go for the offensive rebound, however, there are some things I do to overcome the defensive rebounder's advantage. See them below:

1. I anticipate the shot. I learn my teammates' shooting habits, and how our team's offensive plays flow to the basket. I gather up all the information I can so I can anticipate the shot. I look for the signals that tell me a player is about to shoot, or that a play is going to lead to a shot. As soon as I sense the ball is about to be shot, I slip around my defender and establish rebound position.

2. Follow your shot. If you are the shooter, chase your shots as soon as you complete your follow through. Since you shot the ball, you should have a better feel for where the ball will go than anyone else on the court.

3. Don't help your defender. If you are unable to slip around your defender, he will establish rebounding position and then try to make contact with you. Don't let him. Stand back and don't let him touch you. He won't be able to keep track of you.

4. Use fakes to get in position. A defender will attempt to block all paths around him to the basket. Use body fakes to get him moving in one direction so you can sweep around him in the other. For example, as he turns to make the reverse pivot, move as if you are attempting to beat him in the direction of his pivot. As soon as he speeds up his turn to block you in that direction, sweep around him on the other side.

5. Run out of bounds and come back in under the basket. If you can't get around your defender using fakes, run around him and out of bounds under the basket. Slide back in under the basket and disrupt the defensive team's "blocking out" strategy.

Keeping It Alive—If I can't grab an offensive rebound, I will tip or tap the ball to keep it in the air so I or one of my teammates will have another chance at it.

6. Tip or Tap the ball.
If your defender has established good rebound position by the time the ball hits the rim, all you can do is wait and see how far the ball bounces. If it bounces far enough, you may have a chance at it. You can help yourself some if you can force your way in as close to the basket as possible. But be careful not to push too hard or you will be called for a foul. And don't jump into your man either. But, if you can get a hand on the ball, tip the ball up to the basket. If you can't tip it, tap it out to one of your teammates. You don't have to grab the ball on this end, just keep it alive for the chance at another shot.

7. Shift to defense. If your opponent gets the rebound, don't grab at the ball and risk a silly foul. Wait for him to pivot around, and look for the ball. If your man doesn't protect the ball, you may have a chance to steal it. If you can't steal it, get your hands up and block his passing lanes. You will stop or slow the fast break.

Protecting the Ball—After I grab a rebound, I snap the ball into my body and stick my elbows out.

BOUND!!!

Pro Rebounding Tips

Go after every shot. Consider every shot a miss. Believe that you have a chance to grab a rebound every time a shot is taken.

Go in for offensive rebounds with your hands high. This method will help you avoid pushing fouls.

Power up offensive rebounds. If you are too far away to tip-in a ball off the goal, grab the ball and go up with it immediately. This is a good way to set up a three point play.

Run out of bounds and come back in under the basket. This is a legal move to get offensive rebound position when all else fails.

Maintain good distance between you and the basket when blocking out.

Once you are between your man and the basket, keep your opponent as far away from the basket as you can so there is an area for the ball to drop into, so you can jump forward for the ball.

Fight for the ball. Play as rough as you can within the rules of the game. You must be aggressive to be a good rebounder. This is one area of the game where you should be selfish with the ball. Pretend your name is on it. Take it away from anyone who claims it's his.

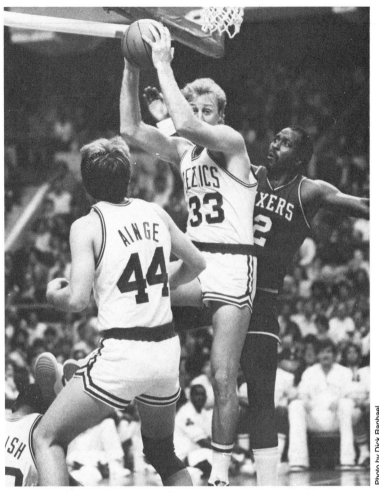

Photo by Dick Raphael

Good Inside Position—As you can see, there's almost nothing an opponent can do to keep you from the ball when you have good inside position.

Photo by Dick Raphael

Looking For The Outlet—As soon as I have control of a rebound, I look for a receiver. I get the ball to him as soon as possible so he can start the fast break.

Photo by Dick Raphael

Blocking Out—When I block out, I establish position far enough from the basket so the rebound will fall between me and the basket.

Practice

1. The Bench Drill—Use a bench for this drill, or string a rope between two objects so that it is about a foot off the ground. Begin the drill standing on one side of the bench or rope with your feet a few inches apart, your knees slightly bent, and your weight concentrated on the balls of your feet.

Jump up and over the bench. Land, and explode off your toes back over the bench. You will need to hold out your arms and establish a jumping rhythm to keep your body in balance. Jump back and forth over the bench for about a minute.

Keep track of how many jumps you make in the minute. The next time you do the drill, work to improve on that number of jumps.

2. Going Up—Start on one side of the basket, and from a semi-crouched rebounding position, explode off your toes and touch the rim with your right hand. Land, and immediately explode off your toes again and touch it with your left hand. Repeat this until you have touched the goal with each hand twenty times. If you can't touch the rim, reach for it. Jump up and extend your hand as far as you can on each jump.

3. The Slap Drill—Grab the ball and hold it over your head, but low enough and in a way that you can allow someone to slap at the ball. Get one of your friends to slap at the ball and try to knock it out of your hands. This will increase your hand strength and keep your opponents from knocking the ball out of your hands when you come down with a rebound.

4. Tip-in—This drill will help keep the ball alive on the offensive board. Begin from the semi-crouched rebound position with the ball in your hands. Begin on the right side of the basket and throw the ball up on the backboard. Follow it up so your right hand makes contact with the ball at the peak of your jump. The fingers of your right hand should be comfortably spread, and you should control the ball with just your fingertips. As your fingertips contact the ball, snap your wrist in a shooting motion, and attempt to bank the ball off the board and into the basket. Repeat this twenty times with your right hand, then move to the left side of the basket and repeat twenty times with your left hand.

5. Back Alley 21—Get together any number of players—two, three, four, five, or more. Play a game to twenty-one, but don't choose teams. Every man will be a team. Every player will have to get his own rebounds and make one-on-one moves to get off a shot. Shoot to see who gets the ball first. The player with the ball works against all the other players to get off a shot. If he hits, he gets to shoot free throws until he misses. Of course, free throws are worth one point and shots from the field are worth two points each.

If the shooter misses a shot or a free throw, it's every man for himself. The player who gets the rebound can put it back up for two. It's a rough game, but it's a great way to learn to anticipate shots, block out, and protect the ball in traffic. It's also a good place to practice powering up shots off rebounds, and tipping in shots. You either learn to do all these things or you don't win Back Alley 21.

I concentrate on and go after every ball that comes off the rim. All good rebounders do.

Photo by Dick Raphael

MOVING WITHOUT THE BALL, AND OTHER CLASS ACTS

"He sees everything you're supposed to see out there.... I'm not saying he's the greatest player, but nobody ever came into this league and played with poise like that. Nobody ever understood the game the way he does."

Red Holzman,
Former Head Coach of the New York Knicks

The stage is set. The lights go up. The players walk on court. Nervous excitement races through the mumbling crowd. A fast paced, four act presentation of "Basketball" is about to begin.

The plot is a simple one. A team of bad guys tries to outwit a team of good guys. Of course, goodness or badness is in the eye of the spectator, and the outwitting is done by the team able to throw a ball through a hoop more times than its opponent. The players who frequently repeat the crowd-pleasing act of sticking leather ball through rope net become heroes of the story. But all players grab a piece of the spotlight. When their parts call for them to dribble, pass, or shoot the ball, 20,000 eyes watch their every move. And if the performer in the limelight scores, half the audience cheers in appreciation. But whether he scores or not, the moment the ball leaves the "headliner's" hand, he's forgotten.

The spotlight pans the ball, and leaves him in the shadows of the game. He's still on the court, but without the ball—his contribution to the scoring effort is hard to see.

Eyes of the audience automatically follow the man with the ball. They watch him bounce, grab, and throw the ball. Each moment he controls it, he holds the promise of bringing his team a fraction closer to victory. But, as in any other production, it takes a lot of people behind the scenes to make a scoring play work. The four players on the edge of the action constantly prepare for the next scene. They may set a pick for the man with the ball, so he is freed to make a crowd pleasing shot. Or, they may scramble their positions on the court in a way that sets the stage for another teammate to play a leading role. The audience will barely notice the upcoming star quickly move to a wide-open spot under the basket. He will just suddenly, magically appear to be in the right place at the right time when the ball hits him in the hands.

Great performances result when players understand their roles so well that they keep one step ahead of the action. Out of the spotlight, they move without the ball and set the stage for themselves or another player to score. When players work hard and move without the ball, a game becomes a real class act.

The Master Mover—*Larry Bird, moving without the ball, cuts downcourt with his eyes wide open and his hands up to receive a pass.*

Photo by Dick Raphael

78

Heeeer weeego—game five, the '81 playoff series, Boston vs. Philadelphia, the Boston Garden, the Celts are down three games to one. With 1:09 remaining, Boston trails 109-106.

All right, Bird takes the inbounds pass from Henderson. He fiddles and diddles, and looks for the open man. Toney comes over. He and Doc double up on Larry. Bird fakes a jumper and flips a one hander to McHale cutting to the hoop. McHale puts up a runner. It's good! And he got fouled on the play!

Folks, the Garden just erupted. Fans are on their feet cheering. What a pass by Bird! What a shot by McHale! Maxwell set a little screen, McHale cut off it, ran down the lane like a runaway freight, and...

McHale tied that game with his free throw, and, of course, the Celtics were on their way to an Eastern Conference title after being down three games to one. The writers and sportscasters naturally pegged McHale and Bird as the last-minute heroes of the crucial fifth game. Bird made the fabulous assist. McHale chalked up the all important three points. But not a line mentioned the fact that Cedric Maxwell's little move without the ball made the game-saving play possible.

The play started with the ball in Bird's hands. Every eye in the Garden was on him. He was expected to make things happen, but he was double teamed. He couldn't get a shot off, and didn't see anyone to pass to. McHale was in pretty good scoring position, but his man was hanging all over him. That's when Maxwell moved up from the other side of the lane and set a screen on McHale's man. That simple play without the ball set the scoring play in motion. McHale saw the screen forming and cut to the basket. Bird saw McHale break free. The rest is history.

A three point scoring play materialized because Maxwell understood the anatomy of a scoring play. He knew if he put himself in the right position at the right time, the "screen and roll" would work for two points.

Larry Bird is basketball's mover without the ball extraordinaire. To him, the basketball court is a great chess board. Each square foot of floor is a game square. Every player, including himself, is a living, breathing, three dimensional chess piece. The pieces move constantly from square to square, but his mind clicks off repeated pictures that show the nine other game pieces frozen in a particular game square at a given instant in time. He instantly analyzes those positions and formulates his strategy.

Number 41 tries to set a pick on me so I can't follow my man as he breaks open for a pass.

Photo by Dick Raphael

He's a chess master. He carefully studies the game board before each move. He moves only one game piece, himself, but by moving himself to strategic positions on the court he creates scoring opportunities for himself and his teammates. He determines each move by making a quick "what if analysis". What if he moves to set a pick on his teammate's defender? Is his teammate looking for the pick? Will the pick free him for a good percentage shot? What happens if he fakes his man and cuts hard to the basket? Is there an open lane available? Will his defender take his fake? Is the man with the ball looking to throw the ball to the open man? What if he has several moves to choose from? Which is the best one? Which is the move without the ball that will put his team in good scoring position?

More often than not the right solution pops into Larry's head. His mind is a high speed basketball computer. It takes in data on speed, position, and direction, and instantly spits out the right scoring play for almost every situation. He's not the biggest, the strongest, or the quickest player in the NBA, but his creative basketball mind puts him in a category by himself.

Here's a basketball tip you can write down and staple to your gym shorts: **NEVER STAND ON THE COURT.** Keep moving on offense, even though you don't have the ball.

If you move without the ball, you can get yourself open for good percentage shots; you can set screens and picks for your teammates, and free them for good shots; moving ahead of the action will put you in good defensive rebounding position. And besides making those things possible, your movement without the ball will keep the defense busy, and may confuse them just enough to give you the edge you need.

You should keep moving on the court, but that doesn't mean you wander around the court aimlessly. It means you make moves that will help your team score. To be able to choose these moves, however, you need to understand what's happening on the court. You need to use your knowledge of the game to analyze players' moves and positions on the court. That's the only way you can intelligently choose your next move without the ball.

I move well without the ball because I have become a student of the game. I study my teammates' and opponents' playing styles. I learn what every player's favorite shots are. If a player makes the same fakes every time he shoots, I make a mental note. And the way a defender guards his man is very important to me, too. I want to know if a defender plays a few feet off his man or plays him toe to toe. I want to know if he's alert, and works at playing defense, or whether he loses his concentration and just goes through the motions. I fill my mental notebook up with all kinds of facts.

Start taking your own notes on player's habits. If you see that a particular guard always takes the shot when he's open in a spot just to the right of the top of the key, remember that. If there's a big man who always looks to pass the ball, unless he has a wide open shot two feet out, use that information. Move in position for a pass and give him a target. The more you know about the players in the game, the better you will be able to anticipate. You will be able to move without the ball and get yourself in the right place at the right time. **LOOK, LISTEN, AND LEARN** from your opponents and teammates.

Listen To Your Teammates

After you play a few minutes with any group of players, you should notice that each player has a way of telling you what his next move will probably be. He doesn't speak right up and say, "I'm going to put up a shot"; but by the way he tilts his head toward the basket, or by the way he begins to coil for a jump shot, he tells you everything you need to know.

Here are a few things your teammate's actions will tell you if you learn to listen:

- When your teammate moves toward one of his favorite shooting positions on the court he's saying, "I'm probably going to shoot, so get in offensive rebounding position."

- If your teammate is closely guarded, he's saying, "Set a pick or screen on my man so I can get free for the shot."

- If your teammate moves so that he opens a passing lane between you, he's saying, "Look for the pass."

- Your teammate may set a pick or screen on your defender even though you don't have the ball. If he does, he's saying, "Cut off my pick or screen to the basket, or cut to the man with the ball for a pass."

- If your teammate gets trapped by defenders without a dribble, he's saying, "Cut to me for the ball. Move toward me, and give me a passing target so I can get rid of the ball."

- If your teammate rarely shoots, even when he has an open shot, he's saying, "When I get the ball, work to get open for a pass."

- Anytime your teammate gets the ball, he's saying, "Work to get open in good shooting position, and hold out your hand, and give me a good target to hit."

Listen To Your Opponent

Your defensive man will attempt to keep you from doing what you want to do. If you want to get open to receive a pass, he'll try to block your passing lanes. If you want to get in offensive rebounding position, he'll try to block you out. But the funny thing is that if you study your defender carefully enough, he'll tell you exactly how to get open for passes and gain position for rebounds.

Here are a few examples of what a defender will tell you if you learn to listen:

- When a defender plays several feet off me, he's saying either, "I don't think you're much of an offensive threat," or "I don't think I can control you if I move in much closer." Move to an open passing lane, receive the pass, and you will be open for a shot.

- If a defender plays you tight, he's saying, "You'll have to give me a good fake or cut off another player if you want to get open."

- When you pass the ball to a teammate and your defender watches the flight of the pass, he's saying, "Cut behind me to the basket, and you'll be wide open for the pass and a lay-up."

- When you fake to the left and your defender lunges left, he's saying, "Your fake worked; now cut around me to the right."

- When you fake to your left and your defender doesn't move, he's saying either, "I don't believe your fake," or "I wasn't ready for it." Try to go hard left, or try another fake.

- If your defender likes to block shots, he's saying, "Give me a good ball fake, and I'll go up for the block. Get me up in the air and you can do as you wish."

- If your defender is slow getting back on defense, he's saying, "Hustle down to your offensive end, and you'll be open for a long outlet pass."

Cutting To The Ball—*Kevin McHale is stopped on the baseline, so I cut to the ball from the weak side and give Kevin a target to pass to.*

RK Hubbard Photo

Moves To Make

It's important to pay attention to your teammates' and opponents' moves on the court, but it's not enough for you to sit back and take in all that information. You've got to use it. Basketball is a fast paced game. Opportunities come and go in the blink of an eye. Use your knowledge of the game to decide your next move, and make it, immediately.

Here are some moves you can make when the time is right:

Fakes—Use head, shoulder, eye, hand, and foot fakes. Fakes get your defensive man moving in the direction opposite to where you really want to go. But to make your fakes work, you must:

- Make your last fake in the direction opposite the direction you want to go.

- Make your fake believable. If you fake left, put enough energy into it so your defender will believe you really are going left.

- Make your fake at 3/4 speed. Save a little speed for your final burst away from your defender.

- Watch your defensive man to see how he reacts to your fakes. Use your peripheral vision to see if your fakes work, or whether you need to try another.

Cut offs—If you can't get free of your defender, run past players standing on the court, and cut hard around them, or through them, and leave your defender behind.

The V-Pattern Move—A good defensive man will work to stay between you and the basket. When you get to the basket, he'll retreat to maintain his position. Take advantage of this by making the V-pattern move:

• Run to the basket at 3/4 speed.

• Plant one foot just before you reach the basket.

• Charge back to the man with the ball.

• Receive the pass, pivot, and then pass or shoot the ball.

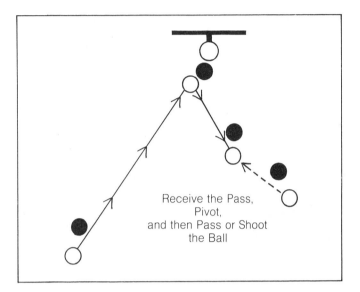

Receive the Pass,
Pivot,
and then Pass or Shoot
the Ball

Make A Target—*I hold up my hand to give the passer a safe target to pass to.*

A variation on the V-pattern is the hook pattern. To make it, drive your defender to the basket the same way you did to make the V-pattern move, but instead of planting your foot and driving back to the man with the ball, follow a path shaped like a fishhook. It's a path that will take you to the basket and around a sharp curve that brings you back to the man with the ball.

Make a target—Make yourself a good target for a pass. When a man guards you close enough to shut off the passing lane between you and the man with the ball, hold your hand out away from your defender and give the passer a good target. Keep your body positioned between your defender and the target to keep the passing lane open.

Anticipate shots—Go for the basket as soon as you know a shot is going up. You can anticipate shots if you study your teammates, and learn the clues that tell you they're going up for a shot.

Set picks and screens for your teammates—When you set a pick or screen, all you do is position your body in the way of a defender so he can't follow the man he's guarding. It won't take you long to understand the fundamentals of setting picks and screens, but it will take a lot of game experience to learn the right place and the right time to set them. Ask your coach to help you with this.

To set a pick:

• Anticipate. Look at the way players are positioned on the court. Set a pick if you can see that it will free your teammate to move into good shooting position, or see it will free him to break open to receive a pass.

• Run up to your teammate's defensive man so that your chest is in front of his shoulder. You might even barely touch his shoulder with your chest. You should set your feet in a wide stance, and keep your arms down at your sides.

• Your teammate should then cut right past you so close that you brush uniforms.

• As soon as you see you have freed your teammate, pivot, and "roll" to the basket, and get in rebound position.

Many times the man guarding you will "switch off" on the man you have just freed in order to help his teammate protect the basket. If he does, you should be open for a pass when you "roll" to the basket. This play, "the pick and roll," is the most fundamental offensive play in basketball.

Help out a teammate in trouble—When you see a teammate trapped by a defender without a dribble, cut toward him, then circle around him, holding your hand out to give him a target. Make fakes, or whatever moves you must to open a passing lane to him.

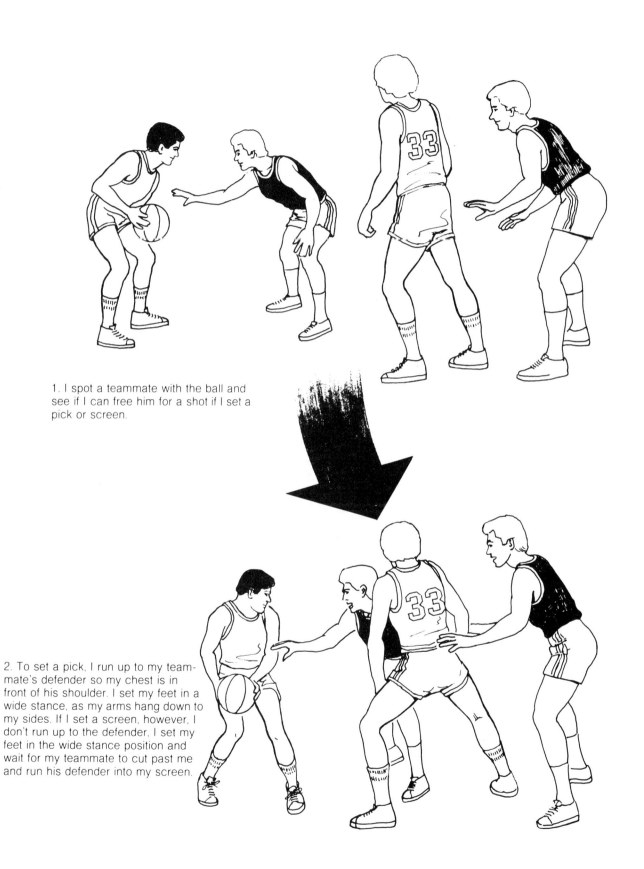

1. I spot a teammate with the ball and see if I can free him for a shot if I set a pick or screen.

2. To set a pick, I run up to my teammate's defender so my chest is in front of his shoulder. I set my feet in a wide stance, as my arms hang down to my sides. If I set a screen, however, I don't run up to the defender, I set my feet in the wide stance position and wait for my teammate to cut past me and run his defender into my screen.

4. If my defender switches off and picks up my teammate, I "roll" to the basket. In the situation below, I pivot on my right foot, move out from between both defenders, and cut to the basket. Neither defender is in good defensive position to cover me as I move to the basket.

3. After my feet are set, my teammate will cut past my shoulder so that I block out his defender with my body. This should free my teammate long enough for him to shoot a jump shot.

Open Man—*If I am the open man closest to the basket, I go up with the shot.*

Moving With The Ball

Most moves without the ball are designed to get you open for passes. So, once you have the ball, what are you going to do? Some passes will hit you wide open in good percentage areas of the court, and you'll be able to go right up with the shot. Other times, however, your defender is going to clamp down on you and maybe even get some help from a teammate. In this case, you're going to have to decide your next move with the ball.

When I get the ball, there is a checklist of moves with the ball that I run through my head. The checklist below shows my first, second, third, and fourth choices. Whenever I get the ball:

- The first thing I want to do is shoot the ball if I am the open man closest to the basket.

- If I am not the open man closest to the basket, I want to pass the ball to the man who is.

- If I have neither a good shot to take, nor an open man to pass to, I fake my man, and move to a position on the court from which I can shoot or pass the ball.

- I look to move the ball toward the basket as in choices one, two, and three, but if I can't move the ball toward the basket, I pass the ball into the backcourt. Then I will either set a pick or screen for the man I passed to, or will set one to free one of my other teammates for the pass.

Photo by Dick Raphael

Jump Pass—*If I'm not the open man closest to the basket, I pass off to the teammate who is.*

Photo by UPI

Now you see it—*I fake a move with the ball to get my defender moving in one direction.*

Photo by UPI

Now you don't—*As soon as I see, with my peripheral vision, that my defender has shifted his weight in the direction of the fake, I pass the ball down the open passing lane I created with my fake.*

Look For Defensive Mistakes

No matter what you want to do with the ball, you can bet a defender won't be more than a couple of steps away. His job is to distract you and force you into a ball handling error or at least to force you into a poor percentage shot.

Remember, though, that as long as you control the ball, you have a slight advantage on your defender. You know what you're going to do next. He doesn't. He has to respond to each move you make, because you are a threat. You can score points. So, all the time you have the ball, make your defender work. Constantly move and fake him. Force him into a defensive mistake.

Here are some defensive mistakes I look for:

- I look to see if a defender plays too far off of me. If he does, I know he can't be a threat to my jump shot.
- I look to see if a defender looks away from me, or is otherwise distracted. If he loses his concentration, I take off for the basket.
- I look to see if a defender lunges at my fakes and gets his weight too far forward. If he gets off balance in this manner, my fakes will be very effective, and I can easily drive around him.
- I look to see if a defender's knees are bent or straight. If they're straight, I know he's not ready to play defense. I can do what I want.
- I look to see how a defender handles the "pick and roll." If he becomes confused and doesn't switch smoothly, I set picks and force him into making a mistake.
- I look for any weakness in my opponent's game. If he has a hard time guarding me when I drive to the right, I will drive to his right every time I get the ball, until he overplays to correct his mistake. Then I can fake to the right and go left. I can mix up my plays and keep him completely off balance.

Moves To Make

Fakes—Use fakes to move the ball, just as you used them to move without the ball. If you really want to drive to the basket, you might get your man off balance by faking a shot. Bring the ball up toward shooting position just as if you were going to shoot, but as soon as you see your defender take your fake, and he has shifted his weight toward you, put the ball on the floor and head to the basket.

Picks and Screens—Just as you set picks and screens for your teammates, they will set them for you. When they do, drive off your teammate's hip in the direction opposite the path he took to set the pick. Cut past him so close that your uniforms brush. Don't give your defender any room to slip through the pick.

Remember, too, if your teammate's defender switches off on you, look for your teammate "rolling" to the basket. He should be wide-open.

Faked out—My head, eye and body fakes got my defender off his feet. If I go straight up for the shot I will probably draw the foul. If I still have my dribble I can drive around him to the basket.

Using the Screen—I get ready to cut past Robert Parish's right shoulder so my defender can't follow me to the basket.

1. I fake the shot.

2. My defender goes for the fake and gets off his feet.

3. I am patient and wait for my defender to glide past.

4. I go up for the shot before he reestablishes good defensive position.

The Pivot—If you get caught in close to the basket without the dribble, and without an open shot, you still have one move.

Even though you can't dribble, you can move by pivoting on one foot. To pivot, you just turn on the ball of one foot by picking up your other foot and throwing your body weight in the direction you want to go. Just make sure you don't lift your pivot foot. With this move, you may be able to move away from your defender just enough to get off a shot or a pass.

The Give and Go—Pass the ball to a teammate, and cut to an open area of the court for a return pass. The give and go is that simple, but proper timing of the move is the key to its success.

It will be a natural tendency of your defender to relax and lose some of his concentration when you give up the ball. After all, he has been working hard to keep you from scoring; and when you pass the ball he will feel he has done his job. The instant you sense his loss of concentration, take off with a burst of speed to an open area of the court. Use your hands to make a good target for the passer.

The Crossover—The crossover step allows you to drive around either side of your defender. The important thing to remember about this move is that your first step to the basket will be made with the same foot no matter which direction you want to drive. If your pivot foot is your left foot, you will make your first step to your right or left with your right foot.

If you want to drive to your right, simply kick out your right foot and step around the right side of your man in the direction of the basket. If you want to drive left, cross your right leg in front of your body, and make your step around your defender's left side and as much toward the basket as possible.

Stop and Pop—To pull off the "stop and pop" you must be able to dribble at full speed, stop instantly, and go up for the jumper before your defender recovers.

Prepare for the quick stop by balancing your body weight a little back of your body's center line. Slap the full sole of your forward foot (time your step so your forward foot is the foot of your shooting hand) on the floor and bend the knee of that leg to absorb your forward momentum. As you begin your step, pick the ball up off the dribble with both hands, and hold it in close to your body. Be patient and don't go up for your shot until you square off with the basket, and make sure your body is balanced. Make your moves quickly but methodically.

A Tough Situation—What move would you make?

Photo by Dick Raphael

IT TAKES A TEAM

Photo by Dick Raphael

"Larry knows how to relate to his teammates. He comes to play hard every night, and that takes away everyone else's excuse not to. He is a silent leader. He doesn't get out in front of us and lead, instead, he stays with us."

M.L. Carr, Boston Celtic player

It's beautiful, the way the five fingers of a hand reach out as one, and automatically, effortlessly do what they must do, so the hand can grasp and turn a door knob, or pick up and hold a water glass. The five players of a basketball team should display the same coordinated oneness. And when they do, that too, is beautiful.

The people yelled and the sound came at us like waves and the first half was tough and then as the final quarter began it was fantastic. I put my hand up and a ball was in it and I threw to Sam Jones. I put my hand out and there was another ball and I threw to K.C. Jones and he made it. I put my hand out and there was another ball and I threw to Havlicek and he made it. I threw and threw and blocked and threw and the team—the world champion Boston Celtics—was a team. Every game we played meshed together and we didn't even know we were shutting them out. We just knew shoot, run, block, pass, shoot.

From Go Up For Glory by Bill Russell as told to William McSweeny

Players of the Celtic dynasty teams of the late Fifties and all of the Sixties meshed like the gears of a precision machine. Not every single minute they played, but that select group enjoyed more of those rare moments when the five played as one than any other assembled quintet in the history of the game.

Russell, Cousy, Sharman, Heinsohn, Ramsey, Sam Jones, K.C. Jones, Sanders, Havlicek—they were some of the greats who melded their talents to create the greatest teams in basketball history. They each clearly understood the purpose of the team, which was winning, and their particular part in that purpose, which was whatever the team needed them to do for it to win. And in case a player happened to forget, Arnold "Red" Auerbach was there to make ice clear in a player's mind what that *whatever* should be.

Bill Russell came to the Celtics from the University of San Francisco in 1956. His credentials were that of an awesome defensive center. Numerous times he had single-handedly demoralized his alma mater's court foes with his uncanny shot blocking ability. The rest of the book on him, however, read that he wasn't much of a shooter. In fact, the only shot he had any confidence in was his dunk shot.

So when Russell entered the NBA, he felt he had something to prove. He wanted to show he could be more than an intimidating defender. He wanted to show he could be a big scorer, too. In practice, he began launching his version of the jump shot from fifteen and twenty feet out.

His shots fell from the rim and backboard like wounded ducks. But they didn't fall for long. Auerbach walked into the gym and blasted at him from across the floor, "Russell, what the hell are you doing shooting from out there besides making a fool of yourself?" Right then and there it was made perfectly clear to Mr. Russell that he hadn't been signed to a pro contract so he could learn to throw the ball in the basket from twenty feet.

Auerbach didn't want Russell fooling around doing something he didn't do well. It was his job as coach to mold a winning team out of the odds and ends of talent he had assembled. He knew to do that he had to use that talent in a special way. He wanted his best shooters to shoot the open shots; his best rebounders to rebound; and his best ball handlers to handle the ball. Of course, he wanted well-rounded players who could contribute some shooting, passing, and rebounding to a winning effort; but he wanted each player to concentrate on giving the most of his best.

If Russell, a poor shooter, took the fifteen and twenty foot shots, he would be contributing his worst talent— not his best. He would waste one of his team's precious opportunities to score each time he took a shot from that range. And even if he developed his shooting touch, his concentration on shooting would only throw the team out of balance. There were already players on the team to fill the scoring roles. If he became intent on shooting, he wouldn't be able to focus his efforts on picking for, passing off to, and rebounding for the good shooters—the things he did best—the things his team needed him to do.

Every player who joins the Celtics today, just as every player who joins any other team, must learn the same lesson as Mr. Russell. No matter how great a player may be, he must learn there are some basketball skills he performs better than others. Even a player like Larry Bird, who has been called the most complete player ever, must realize he can't do it all, all of the time. He must realize that the guards on the team handle the ball better than he does, or that another player is a better defensive player. And even though he may be a great shooter, he must realize that some nights he'll go cold or one of his teammates will get hot, and he will need to give up the shot to another. He must realize he is a piece of a puzzle called a team. If he is a player like Larry Bird, he is a big piece and shapes his game so he contributes considerable shooting, passing, and rebounding skills to the picture. But he may also be a small piece of the picture, and contribute mainly rebounding and defensive skills. It's not so important what a player contributes, but that he knows how he fits into the team picture. Because each piece is as important as every other, it takes all the pieces to make a team.

Teamwork—it's the name for the coordinated mix of talent, desire, and intelligence that makes a team a team. It's the special ingredient that allowed the Boston Celtics to dominate the NBA for a decade. It's the careful mixture of thought and action that gives any team the potential to be a winner. Teamwork, after all, is implied in the word team. Every coach knows that. Every one knows it his job to form a cohesive unit out of his players. Of course, that's a difficult task in any sport; however, it doesn't take much investigation to discover that teamwork is more difficult to achieve in basketball than in any other sport.

Take football, for example. It's so well organized that a player knows exactly what he has to do so his team will work.

The idea in football is to move the ball across the goal line. Eleven men must work together to do it. Each one is assigned a specific role—lineman, quarterback, end—and he performs his specific role according to a rehearsed script called a playbook. For example, the quarterback calls out "X-20 slant on three"; and the tight end knows that on three he will slant off the line at a forty-five degree angle, put down his head, and knock over a linebacker. That's all. And when every other player on the team executes his role correctly (execution is a key word in football), the team works, and the eleven-man machine rumbles down the field in a cloud of dust.

Baseball is a game of positions. The field is shaped like a diamond. Within that diamond are bases, fields, a plate, and a mound. A player is assigned a particular position. He's a baseman, fielder, pitcher, catcher. Every player takes his turn at being a batter.

Most work done by the team is done when it's in the field, on defense. Nine players play defense while one batter tries to score. Each defender stands in his position and waits for the ball to come to him. When it does, he applies his special skill to it. He catches it and stands on his base; he catches it and throws it to the infield; he catches it and hurls it to the catcher; he catches it and tosses it back to the pitcher. Of course, the one man on offense swats at it with his bat.

There are rare moments when players have to think about how they will react to each other's actions and reactions—the double play, the pick off, the run down, the back up. But generally the team works well when each player does a good job of applying his skill to the ball when it comes his way.

Soccer and hockey are fluid, free-wheeling games like basketball. All the players have a more or less equal chance to kick or head the ball, or slap the puck with their stick. Also, like basketball players, soccer and hockey players must learn to sense and react to the moves and positions of their teammates. Unlike basketball, however, the odds in both games are against scoring. Scores of 1-0 or 2-1 are common. A team must angle the ball past ten defenders before it can take a shot on goal. And at that point, there is still a player, the goalie, permanently stationed in front of the goal. There is no doubt the effort of ten men is required if a team is to have a chance of slipping the scoring object through a crease in the defense and into the goal. The sheer difficulty of scoring forces the players to work together as a team.

Then there is basketball. Rehearsed plays don't work well in this game. The action is too fast. Teams don't start from a dead stop. They can't go back and huddle when a play doesn't work.

Positions don't mean much in basketball. Whether a player is called a guard, forward, or center, he has the same potential to dribble, shoot, pass, rebound, or perform any other game skill.

And it's the game in which each team is likely to score a goal every minute. Scoring is far from difficult. A player can make a dandy one-on-one move and always get off some kind of shot. He doesn't need to work with his teammates to score. It just works out for the best if he does.

So what it boils down to is this: the magical balance of effort that constitutes teamwork is in the hands of the individual players. And, for the most part, these are players who learned the basic skills on their own. They spent hours shooting at the goal. They played in a hundred odd pick-up games, games in which winning and losing were less important than scoring and looking good doing it. These are the raw units of basketball talent a coach must teach to work as a team: players who respond to having the ball in their hands by putting up a shot.

But despite the way a player grows up with the game, if he wants to be a winner, he must learn to be a team player. It will require great effort, intelligence, and maturity on his part. And even then his desire to do it on his own—to score a lot of points—will always be lurking there in the back of his mind. But he must keep thinking and:

1. Know what his strengths and weaknesses are.
2. Know what his teammates' strengths and weaknesses are.
3. Know how teammates must work together to set up scoring plays.
4. Know every minute what skills he should contribute to the effort.

It takes time. But when a player understands what teamwork is about, the game opens up before him. He can see scoring plays as they develop. He knows they materialize when offensive players cluster in particular ways. Two cluster—one player picks for another. Three cluster—teammates cluster along a line and zip the ball back and forth between each other until one can slice through the two man defense to the basket. More cluster—a series of screens and passes frees a man for a wide-open shot under the basket.

He can see, he can sense from the clues—the angle of a cut, player's positions on the court, the flight of the ball—a scoring play becomes a picture in his mind. The cluster forms in his mind a split second before it does on the floor and he knows if he is to be the shooter, passer, picker, or rebounder. He sees. He moves—constantly. He and his team are one. He knows exactly what both of them must do to win.

Photo by Dick Raphael

One of Dr. J's high-flying "slam jams" or one of my three-point "rainbows" gets the fans on their feet cheering, but it takes more than a few spectacular individual plays to win a game. It takes a team.

Teams work, teams score when players know how to move without the ball and set up high percentage shots. Teams work when players look to pass the ball to the open man closest to the basket. Teams work when all five players on the team know what role they need to play for the team to win.

Not every player can lead the team in scoring; but just because you aren't a big scorer doesn't mean you are any less important to the team. Picking for shooters, picking so others can get rebounds, working to get in good offensive rebounding position are skills as important to winning as shooting the ball. So are switching on defense, double-teaming, and rebounding on the defensive end. There are many little things that have to be done if a team is going to win, and your job is to find which of them your team needs you to do. Then you must do them well.

Your coach will tell you what he expects you to contribute to the team. He may expect you to lead the team in scoring. He may expect you to play every minute of the game. He may expect you to be the all purpose "sixth" man and come in off the bench to give the team a boost. He may expect you to sit the bench, and serve as a practice player for the starters.

Whatever your role, do your best. If you think your role should be bigger, that you have more to contribute to the team, show your coach in practice. That's the place to prove yourself. Don't complain if you're not happy with your role. Don't talk down other players. Above all, you must have respect for your teammates and the decisions of your coach. The players of the team, the coach, and the manager must be bonded by a mutual respect.

There's no way you will be best of friends with every player on the team, but when you're on the floor, treat all your teammates as if they were your best friends. Leave any differences you have in the locker room. Thank a teammate for a good pass. Give him "five" for a good shot. Tell him that he made a great play. Everybody likes to be told they've done a good job.

Learn to work with your teammates, and you will experience the great things teamwork can do. I've been lucky to play on great teams in high school, college, and now in the pros. And one of the best examples of what can happen when a team works together, I experienced when I was a senior at Indiana State University. Our team was picked to finish fourth in the Missouri Valley but ended up going all the way to the final game of the NCAA championships.

Our team wasn't loaded with talent, but we had enough and used it in the right way. We had Brad Miley who couldn't shoot from out, but could rebound and defense any player in the country. We had Carl Nicks, who was raw power and hustle. He shot and led the fast break. We had Alex Gilbert who specialized in rebounding. We had other players who added other specialties to the effort. And the team worked because everybody knew what was expected of them. Every player gave his best. The team won.

And take it from me, there is no greater victory than a team victory. You know at the end how much all the guys worked and sacrificed for that moment. It's the greatest feeling in the world.

◁ **Out-of-Bounds Play**—*I have 5 seconds to get the ball back in bounds to an open teammate.*

THE MAN THEY CALL COACH

"The strength of the group is in the strength of the leader. Many mornings when I am worried or depressed, I have to give myself what is almost a pep talk, because I'm not going before that ball club without being able to exude assurance. I must be the first believer, because there is no way I can hoodwink the players."

Vince Lombardi

How does one describe the man who stalks the sidelines of each game like a caged tiger? Psychotic, neurotic, manic-depressive, and hysterical are some of the labels that have been pinned on him from time to time. But what he really is, is a kind of human chameleon. Depending on the need or situation, he can change himself to fill the role of father figure, strategist, executive, administrator, public relations man, psychologist, travel agent, or teacher, to name a few. And depending on how his team fares on the basketball court, he can turn from a serene, well-mannered gentleman into a crimson-faced, wildly gesticulating madman. He lives a life that pulls him apart. He rides an emotional roller coaster through game after game. His heart races. Acid juices gnaw at his stomach. But the man they call coach risks psychological disturbance and physiological destruction because, in addition to his other emotional quirks, he's obsessed with winning basketball games.

Three fine specimens of winners—John Wooden, Al McGuire, Bobby Knight—the stern schoolmaster, The hustler, the General Patton of college coaching. The first two have dropped out of the rat race—big time college coaching. The third is still racing.

In his day, John Wooden guided his UCLA Bruin teams to an unprecedented ten NCAA championships. He obediently rode the bench through every contest he coached, the only outward sign of his inner tension being the rolled up program clasped in his hand, tapping his knee. But he had to set a good example, because the gymnasium was his classroom, and he considered himself its headmaster. When he conducted basketball practice, he lectured as much on character as on basketball and winning. *Psychology Today* magazine even researched and reported on his successful coaching style. They believed there was something in this teaching methods that could be of value in more academic settings. That delighted him.

His manner was straightforward. He praised and scolded his players as he drilled them in the fundamentals. To him, basketball was a precise science that demanded efficient execution of the game's basic skills. He taught his players the fundamentals of shooting, passing, dribbling, rebounding and defense to give them a foundation on which they could build their basketball careers; he taught them industriousness, cooperation, confidence, concentration, and team spirit to give them a foundation on which to build their lives.

Al McGuire never sat the bench. He preferred to rage at the officials from the sidelines. He tried to grab hold of the game with his clipped Noo Yawkese commands and traffic cop hand signals. Sometimes he grabbed too hard. In one memorable game he was whistled for a technical foul that cost his Marquette Warriors a shot at an NCAA crown.

When the coach calls a huddle, everybody listens.

Photo by Dick Raphael

He referred to himself as a "depression baby" and was forever pinching himself to make sure his success was for real. And because he never forgot where he came from, he could carry on no nonsense streetwise dialogues with his intercity recruits. His style was "right on" with them. He didn't believe Marine haircuts and strict curfew built character. He didn't believe in blackboards or too much organization. He thought basketball was just a game and should be fun to play. And if he used it to teach anything, he used it to teach survival in the cruel world.

His practices were sometimes disrupted by two players resolving their differences through knuckle diplomacy. He stood back and let them go at it. He thought it was best to let the sore spots between players fester and heal naturally. He thought bringing things out in the open brought the team together in the end.

And his teams, year after year, did have a kind of street gang cohesion that allowed them to consistently out perform the sportswriters' pre-season predictions. They scraped and clawed their way to winning seasons. They displayed the gritty determination McGuire would want them to use to scrap their way in the cruel world. Because, as he would say, "There's no free lunch." But still, he gave them a boost when they left Marquette. He helped them grab onto the ropes. He hyped his star players and wheeled and dealed to land them lucrative pro contracts. He did what he could for the rest. He sent his players off with their eyes wide-open, looking for the angle, the payoff, the price.

Bobby Knight is the current big winner, sometimes philosopher, on the big-time college circuit these days. He mixes scrunching in his chair with raging at the officials.

When he's not sitting in his chair, he sometimes kicks it. And when kicking and scrunching won't do, he may grab a handfull of one of his Indiana Hoosier players' jerseys and proceed to let him know that all is not well.

Nobody has to tell you that his heroes are people like General Patton and Harry S. Truman, and that he started his coaching career at a school like West Point. He wears military exactitude and a kind of tough-talk attitude like he wears his red plaid sport coat. He's a taskmaster. He growls at his players in true military fashion and motivates them with patented foot-in-the-seat-of-the-pants methodology. Basketball is his tool. Discipline is his lesson. He demands that his players do what they're supposed to do; when they're supposed to do it; every time they're supposed to do it. That's what he expects them to do on the basketball court. That's what he expects them to do in life.

Basketball under Knight is four years of boot camp, yet the players who make it through his basic training look back and realize they never had a better teacher, never had a better friend.

Three giants of college coaching, three dynamic personalities, three philosophies of coaching that spill over into life—beneath each of the three thick skins, however, there lurks the same king-sized ego. Each of them could look any man in the eye and say, "Follow me. I know what success is. I can lead you to victory." Their words were strong, because their faith in themselves is stronger. It has to be for them to weather the losses that threaten to dishearten them. It has to be for them to resist the pressures from all sides that must tempt them to adopt a win-at-all-costs mentality. Against the odds, they succeed in a hellish profession without compromising their values. They fulfill their highest responsibility, that of providing a model for the young people with whose guidance they are entrusted.

A twist in their characters, an incident in their past, something made them leaders instead of followers. It was their simple love of the game, though, that turned them into coaches. They grew up with the game. Wooden was a standout All-American at Purdue. McGuire played a stint of pro ball. Knight played on the same Ohio State championship team as John Havlicek. Each of them came to the end of his time or talent as a player before he was done with the game. To their kind, though, basketball was more than a game.

Basketball is a tiny country in a big chaotic world. It's a country with its own rules and regulations—its own values and rewards. Life around the hardwood smacks of something old, of something traditional. There is glory and honor there. Young men are asked to dig deep down into themselves to give their all to defeat a common foe. Leaders are still followed and respected there. Courage in the face of adversity is expected. Iron discipline can be demanded without question. The camaraderie of a group of individuals working, struggling, sacrificing can be found there, too. And at the end of the struggle there is always the opportunity to feel the exhilaration of total victory, a feeling heightened by the equal possibility of total defeat. At the end of their playing days, Wooden, McGuire and Knight weren't ready to leave such a country.

Father figure, strategist, executive, administrator, public relations man, psychologist, travel agent, and teacher—it has been said before that the coach pays the highest price to enjoy the rewards of the sport. He must doff and don a rack full of hats each day. He must answer to the fans, players, administration, alumni, townspeople, and the media. The pressure comes from all sides. He has no place to hide. His record is there for all to see. Yet, the true measure of a coach is, perhaps, an accomplishment that may or may not be visible on the basketball court.

It was Heywood Hale Broun who said, "Sports don't build character, they reveal it." And if that statement is true, the highest purpose of coaching is revealed therein. The coach must be above all else a consummate teacher. He certainly must teach the game, but more importantly he must teach each of his players about himself. He must teach him to set and achieve goals. He must lead him to the limits of his potential so he knows the feeling of doing the best that he can. He must teach him to unselfishly give his talents so they best serve the needs of the team. He must teach him how to win.

Wooden, McGuire, and Knight—great coaches, respected teachers. Their lasting legacies are not their win-loss records or their championships, but the potentials they unlocked and the character they revealed.

Respect your coach. Listen and learn from him. He is your teacher and leader. When there are only ten seconds left in the game, and your team is down one point, only one man can decide what is to be done, and who is to do it. The coach is a trained professional and knows what must be done. He is in charge and must make the decision to do it. That goes the same for every decision that must be made about game strategy, practice, or anything else to do with the game. Someone must make decisions for the team, and the coach is that someone.

If you want to feel the difference a coach can make, try this. Before fall basketball practice, work out and get in the best shape you can. Then during the first week of practice, feel how sore you are by the third day of practice. That soreness in your muscles is a measure of the difference your coach makes. No matter how far you can push yourself, he can push you a little further. He can get a little more out of you. It's his job to help you perform to the limits of your potential. At times you may hate him for it. He will push you and never let up. He may yell at you or make fun of you. Every coach has his own way. But no matter what he does, remember, he's doing it for a reason. He's preparing you to be the best you can be.

The best way for you to get along with your coach is to want what he wants. Want to win, because that's his job. His job depends on his win-loss record. Want to do whatever you can to help the team. Learn what role the coach wants you to play, because when each player contributes what the team needs, the team wins. Want to practice the fundamentals of the game over and over again. The more skills you have, the more you can contribute to your team. Want your team to succeed more than you want yourself to succeed. To the coach, except for his family, the team is the most important thing in his life.

I worked a lot on my own to develop my basketball skills. There was nobody who could have made me put in all the hours practicing I did. But it was my coaches, especially coaches who taught me to be the very best I could be.

View from the Bench—Like all coaches, Coach Jones affects the outcome of every game by the way he times the use of time-outs and substitutions. Much of his work, though, is done before the game starts.

Looking On—*The official must stay on top of the action in order to make the correct call.*

Photo by Dick Raphael

"There are no natural parameters to judge from. No strike zone, no foul line as in baseball. No line of scrimmage as in football. Nothing is black and white."

Earl Strom, NBA official

Basketball of the playground is the game in its purest form—in the fresh air for the fun of it. The game thrives there without time clocks, referees, coaches, or fans. Yet even in a neighborhood game to fifteen by ones, just below the surface of the action, there's acknowledgement of and respect for the rules of the game. There has to be. Without the rules there is no game. They define it. They give it character. They guarantee that it's fair.

The basketball pick-up game is a phenomenon in American sports. Without organization, without scheduling, heated contests spontaneously ignite around hoops across America. There's no other game a player can fall into so easily. A sandlot footballer can't simply head to the local gridiron and expect twenty guys to show up for a game of two hand touch. A baseball player knows he has to make some phone calls to round up seventeen others and enough equipment; otherwise, there isn't a chance of a nine inning contest. And even a tennis buff doesn't think of reserving a court without first finding a worthy opponent. But basketball players think nothing of dribbling off to the court alone. They go expecting some kind of contest to materialize out of thin air—one-on-one, two-on-two, even a full five-on-five. Amazingly, they are seldom disappointed.

Even if no other players show, that's only a slight disappointment to a ball player. He can content himself with just shooting hoops for hours. But still, the odds are somebody will show. Because players of the hoop game belong to a kind of universal fraternity. They

share an addiction to the feeling that comes from launching the ball off their fingertips and seeing it float up over and through the hoop. Once hooked, they naturally gravitate to the goal wherever it may be. And the only thing they crave more than putting the ball up and through the hoop is putting it up over the outstretched fingers of an opponent and through the hoop. That's why a rim and backboard hang on every other garage and barn in the country. That's why at any given time, at any given hoop, one, two, four or more will gather. Teams will be picked. The game will be played. And the game will be essentially fair.

Even though not a player on the court has read the official rule book, he knows the game. It's in his blood, passed down from older brothers and sisters, from dad, from friends. He knows that a ball passing through the goal scores two points, that a player must dribble the ball if he wants to move with it, and that a team whose player last touches the ball before it goes out of bounds loses possession. He slips into the game and moves around in it like an old pair of Levis. He doesn't think or talk much about the rules, because the game is, for the most part, the rules come to life. For instance, there's the rule that requires players to dribble. So they do. If they don't, the game is no longer basketball. Basketball looks the way it does and is played the way it is, because players dribble and otherwise conduct themselves according to the rules.

Besides giving the game identity, there is a particular section of the rules that is used to keep the game under control. Strictly speaking, enforcement of these rules should mean the game looks like basketball only when there is no physical contact. But pushing, shoving, and checking are facts of life in the game. Their presence reveals the fact that the game is somewhat dishonest with itself. Unlike football, which makes an honest, upfront claim to be a down and dirty full contact sport, basketball makes the dishonest, backhanded claim to be a non-contact sport. Of course, that's baloney. And it's that little lie that causes all the trouble. It causes the game to wobble along its way like a bicycle traveling on a tire rim that's not quite true.

In the real world, basketball games fall somewhere between graceful ballets in sneakers and football without pads. But without some contact the game is gutless. Contact—grabbing, banging, shouldering, checking—is visible evidence that a good quantity of desire and determination is pouring into the game. Aggressive play is what it's called; the type of play that gives the game its hard edge.

Too much contact, though, destroys the game. It simply can't survive if the scales tilt in the favor of muscle over skill. Basketball players are, in their own right, artists who skillfully shoot, pass, and dribble the ball. But if a defender can indiscriminately push, hold, or knock them out of their delicate balance, they can't reasonably perform their skills, and the game is no longer fair. Muscle always wins over skill. That's why fouls are called. But who is clever enough to know when contact is a foul and when it is only evidence of good aggressive play?

On the playground, players call their own. Above the gasps for air and shuffling of rubber soles on grit-covered concrete, the cry, "Foul!," periodically rings out. Play stops. The fouled player takes the ball out. Play resumes.

A player simply opens his mouth to announce his judgement that his right to shoot, pass, dribble, or move about on the court has been unfairly impeded. A defender has pushed or slapped him. Other players may not agree. The defender may roll his eyes to the sky in disbelief, but play will stop, and the players will accept the call. They respect the game and realize fouls must be called to keep the game basketball. And it's the nature of the sandlot game that the players of the game share the responsibility of calling the fouls. There's no one else to uphold the rules.

Of course, sandlot games are more wide-open and free wheeling than organized games with officials. Just enough calls are made to keep the game from erupting into a street fight. Players hate to make calls that interfere with the free flow of the action. Winning and losing aren't so important as getting into the feel of the game. Players like the banging underneath, getting away with a little push off as they go up for a shot. They refuse to destroy a great move by making a traveling call, or a great block with a foul call. For the most part, the code of the playground is the no-harm-no-foul creed of the NBA. If a player gets his hand slapped while taking a shot, he should make the foul call. If he gets knocked to the ground or out of bounds in the process of wrestling for rebound position, he'd better dust himself off and forget it.

The honor system of foul calling works unbelievably well. It has to work. And it does because players aren't on the court to harm each other or bicker over technicalities, just to play ball. But still, the call-your-own system requires players to carry some resentment through each game. There are always the players who call "foul" when they're barely touched. A player will get viciously hacked, but while he waits for his defender to admit such an obvious foul, the play goes on, and it's too late for him to make the call. There are always the pushes and the elbows to the gut that can't be called. A player on the other side of the court from the dribbler will make a traveling call. And, always there are the players who get very sensitive to contact when a close game gets down to the end.

Resentment can build up in a game. The simmering pot of physical activity can begin to boil. Tempers can flare. Yet the game seldom boils over into a fight. Rarely does a player pick up his ball and go home. The energy of anger is more than likely turned into the game instead of fists. The game heats up. The action becomes more furious and punishing. Rules are bent, stretched, twisted. Some are ignored. But the game simmers down or ends with one winner, one loser. The underlying respect for the rules, from beginning to end, keeps the game essentially fair and the game essentially basketball.

★　　★　　★　　★　　★　　★

Foul Called—Basketball uniforms are numbered with numerals between 00-55 inclusive, which allows the officials to use one hand to indicate to the scorer's table the uniform number of the player whistled for the infraction.

When the game moves indoors, into school gyms and arenas that seat 20,000 spectators, and becomes an organized event, it loses a little of its free spirit, as does any wild creature when caged. It's not just played for fun anymore, either. It's played for trophies, championships, for school pride, for money. It's played for the entertainment of a few thousand fans. The game becomes so important to so many people for so many reasons, that enforcement of the rules becomes a very serious matter. So serious, in fact, that professionals are hired to insure the rules are followed, and the path to victory is the same for both teams.

There's one official who starts and stops the clock. Another keeps score and records fouls. Two others, floor officials (three in some college conferences), chase the game up and down the court. They are policemen who blow their whistles on infractions of the rules. They are judges who hand down the appropriate awards and punishments in each case. And when these hired officials make sure the clock starts and stops when it should, that the score is correctly reported, and that every player takes only one and a half steps when he drives for a lay-up, the game has been played by the rules. It has been fair. The best team on that particular night has won.

But what a burdensome task it is to insure the game is played by the rules. The men for the job must certainly be honest. They must be knowledgeable of the game, decisive, and in top physical condition. And, surely, they must love the game; otherwise, their career selection is insane. Because there is simply no way all their skill and dedication can match the demands of the game. Basketball, bar none, is the most difficult sport in the world to officiate.

All at once, the floor official must keep track of the clock, the score, offensive men in the free throw lane, contact away from the ball, contact between the man with the ball and his defender, and the manner in which the ball is handled. The floor area is too great, the action too fast for an official to be able to scurry about and be in the right position to make every call. A ball will be knocked out of bounds. He must make a call. He calls "blue ball" when he should have called "white." A player blocked his view of the play. On another play, he calls a hacking foul, but if he had only viewed the play from a few degrees to the right, he could have seen there was really no contact at all. But you can bet someone in the stands had the right angle. The shouts and boos will let him know that.

But, every official accepts the fact that mass ridicule is there in the stands waiting to pour down on him every time he makes a mistake. There is no place for him to hide when he makes his "judgement call." He must decide right and wrong on the spur of the moment. He must always carry the applicable rules and appropriate punishment for their violation on the edge of his mind. But, before blowing his whistle, he must first draw an imaginary line. On one side of the line, contact is a foul. On the other, it is aggressive but acceptable play. Or, one player crosses the line first, and he calls "charging." If the other crosses first, he calls "blocking." Still he is only

human and doesn't draw the line in precisely the same place every time. He gets tired like everybody else and makes a mistake. He can't always be in the right position. The ridicule, the abusive language seeps through his objectivity and affects his decision. Fallable human judgement becomes another factor in the game like the lucky bounce of the ball.

So calls are made. Calls are missed. The referee is right. He is wrong. The game wobbles along like a bicycle traveling on a tire rim that's not quite true. Players sit on its seat and peddle. Fans perch themselves on either side of the handle bars. The coach runs along side yelling directions. The referee sits uncomfortably on the center bar of the bike with his hands on the handle grips. He's supposed to keep the bike traveling down the centerline of the road. But because of the bent rim, he can't always make the right decision to keep the bike traveling straight down the road. The bike weaves back and forth across the center line. No one is ever completely happy with the ride. Fans and coaches occasionally yell and scream in his ear. But what infuriates them more than anything is an uneven ride. If the referee dips two feet from the center in favor of one team, he had better cross over and dip two feet in favor of the other. Because as soon as the fans or coaches feel the favor of the official has shifted in favor of an opponent, dissatisfaction spreads through the crowd like wildfire. They let loose the boos and cat-calls. They yell, "Kill the bum!"

Coaches explode at them, fans hiss and boo them, players cast looks of disbelief or disrespect their way, but all swallow the biggest piece of their resentment. They love the game and know the official is the one who, from beginning to end, will keep the game essentially fair and the game essentially basketball.

Respect the rules of the game. Respect the officials whose job it is to uphold those rules. Remember, the rules tell you how the game should be played; respect for them keeps the game fair.

But in order for you to respect the rules, you first must know what they are. Listed below are addresses to which you may send requests for official basketball rule books. Take the time to read and study the rules. Knowledge of the rules will allow you to play the game with intelligence and confidence.

If you understand the rules, you will understand the game. You will also realize how difficult the basketball official's job is. What makes it even more difficult is the speed of the game. In a matter of seconds, a team fast breaks from one end of the court to the other. It's impossible for an official to be in the right position to make every call. Sometimes he's blocked from view of the play by players. But even when he's in position, the call is not always easy for him to make. Take the "charging-blocking foul" call. It's strictly a judgement call. The referee must rule whether or not the defensive man established position before contact was made. But then every contact foul is a judgement call. Officials don't call a foul every time players make contact. If they did, both teams would spend all their time on the free throw line. The referee must draw an imaginary line in his head and say to himself, "On this side of the line, contact is a foul; on the other side, it is good aggressive play, and I will allow it." The referee must sit in judgement of every play; blow his whistle or not; and stand by his decision.

Officials make calls to keep the game fair. But they are human. They miss calls. They make mistakes. But whenever you think an official has made a bad call against you or your teammate, forget it. You'll accomplish nothing if you argue with the referee. He will never change his mind. Many calls are judgement calls. And if he blows his whistle, he has made the judgement that an infraction has been committed. He is a trained professional, and most of the time his decision is correct. But when he makes a mistake, don't argue. Nobody likes to be reminded of their mistakes. Besides, if you argue too much he'll call another foul—a technical foul.

You shouldn't argue with the referees, but you should pay close attention to the way they call the game. Just like every player, every referee has his own way of doing things. All referees, at a particular level of play, use the same rule book, but each has his own way of interpreting the rules. Some officials will allow almost no contact between players. They call a "tight" or "close" game. Others will call the action around the ball "close," yet let a lot of rough play take place away from the ball. Then there are officials who begin the game calling it "close" to let the players know they are in control. As the game goes on, they will allow more contact. Other officials will call the beginning of the game "loose," and let the players dictate the kind of game it will be. Then if the players try to get away with too much "hacking," and the game gets rough, the officials will call the game closer.

Besides deciding what's contact and what's not, referees must use their judgement on special situation calls like the "charging-blocking foul" call. And it seems certain officials like to call such calls one way more than the other. For instance, an official will seem to call more blocking than charging fouls, or the other way around. It also seems that some officials are intimidated by a hometown crowd. And sometimes it seems that an official will get tired at the end of a game and miss more calls than usual. But all these individual differences in referees are things you must judge for yourself. Of course, the best referees, like the best players, are consistent performers; but even they will have their own way of calling the game.

Pay attention to the way a game is called. Adjust your play accordingly. If the referee seems to call more blocking than charging fouls, concentrate more on driving to the basket. If the officials call a "loose" game, play very aggressive defense. If they call a "tight" game, be careful on defense; but work hard, fake, and draw fouls on offense.

Of course, there are many other adjustments you can make in your play according to the way the officials call a game. But you can't make those adjustments, you can't play intelligently unless you understand the rules of the game and how they are used to regulate play. Read the rules. Study them. Know them as well as the officials.

SOURCES FOR OFFICIAL BASKETBALL RULE BOOKS

ELEMENTARY AND HIGH SCHOOL
National Federation of State High School Associations
7 South Dearborn Street, Room 1240
Chicago, IL 60603

COLLEGE
College Athletics Publishing Service
349 East Thomas Road
Phoenix, AZ 85000

AMATEUR
Amateur Athletic Union of the United States
3400 West 86th Street
Indianapolis, IN 46268

PROFESSIONAL
The Sporting News
P.O. Box 56
St. Louis, MO 63166

"He can do it when the game's on the line—that's what Bird's about."

Jerry Sloan, former player and head coach
of the NBA's Chicago Bulls

Larry Bird, Cedric Maxwell, Quinn Buckner, Robert Parish, and Danny Ainge started the game for Boston. But the "chemistry" just wasn't right. Passes went off hands out of bounds. There were more in-and-outs and around-the-rimers than swish shots. Breaks went badly for the Celtics. At the end of the third quarter the Indiana Pacers were up by nineteen.

Coach Bill Fitch shuffled Kevin McHale, Gerald Henderson, and M.L. Carr in and out of the lineup. It didn't matter. None of his combinations worked. It was apparently the Pacer's night. Rookie of the year candidate Clark Kellog was well on his way to a thirty-two point game. He and the rest of the Pacers looked sharp. It wasn't until the fourth quarter that the Boston five threatened. They rallied to cut the lead to twelve. But it looked like Indiana's game again, when the Pacers stormed back to go up by fifteen with 6:47 on the clock.

Then something happened. There was a palpable change in the atmosphere of Market Square Arena. It was like the feeling in the air before a storm. And then it came. Bird stole a pass and took it in for a lay-up. Thirty seconds later he canned a three-pointer from deep in the right corner. With 4:22 left, the Pacer lead was 120-113. Then Bird got fouled going up for a jumper and sank his two free throws. The next time down, Robert Parish drove across the lane and "jammed" one, got fouled, and hit the free throw. With less than a minute to play and only a two point lead, the Pacers worked the ball for a shot which they hoped would ice the game. But the shot they got went a quarter of the way down the basket and popped off the rim to the right side of the court. The ball bounced over Bird's head. He bent himself back in the shape of an "r" to reach for the ball and rip it out of a Pacer's hands. He turned and fired a perfect touchdown pass to M.L. Carr, who slam dunked and tied the game.

The Pacer fans were amazed. And they were more than a little disgusted with their team. But when Larry Bird finally turned from the free throw line, smiled, and gave Robert Parish the "high five" after icing the game with a free throw, they weren't surprised. They weren't at all surprised that Bird scored seventeen points in the fourth quarter, made the key shots, steals, rebounds, and passes that turned an apparent Celtic defeat into a great come-from-behind victory. In fact, a classic Bird performance is what most of the fans in Market Square had paid to see. Larry Bird was the reason the game attendance was three times normal. The fans were there to see a champion.

Fans love their sports, but they love their champions more. They love to sit in the stands and feel the nervous swirl in their stomach as the national anthem is played. When the ball goes up for the tip, they love to feel the rush of adrenalin within them. Their hearts pound. But even more, they love to see the "clutch" performance of a champion. There's something about knowing he has what it takes to get the job done, and then seeing him do it. The fan in his seat thirty rows up can take a share of the pride in the victor's accomplishment home with him.

But the spectator takes more than a measure of pride from a championship performance. He takes away memories. They are Kodacolor snapshots he takes with his mind to freeze great moments in sports. He can recall them whenever he wants to remember what a winner looks like. For instance, he can recall the scene of Bird on the edge of the court, wiping off the bottom of his shoes, getting ready to walk onto the court for the game. Larry's face is emotionless, but there is a glint of determination in his eyes. His manner is shot with confidence. The picture is clear. A winner sets his mind on a goal, knows he can reach it, and won't give up until he achieves it.

Another snapshot comes to mind. It's the one of Bird giving Robert Parish the "high five" the minute he knew the game was won. And as the mind of the fan recalls the scene, his body again experiences a share of the powerful, satisfying feeling that goes with the "winning." He sees the champion in his moment of glory and wonders what it would be like to stand in those shoes. But even in his daydream, he knows he'll never fill them. He knows Bird was born with a certain gift for the game. He knows the hard work and sacrifice it took to develop that gift into a profession. He knows Bird stands in the middle of the picture at the end of the game because he has paid victory's high price.

Fans flock to see Larry Bird play basketball because they love his displays of excellence. Nobody touches the game like he does. But for more than that reason,

Photo by Dick Raphael

That Winning Feeling—*Bird enjoys another NBA victory. It's his payoff for years of hard work and forty-eight minutes of all out effort.*

they follow him because they recognize him as a winner. And where there is a winner, there is the "winning." And where there is the "winning," there is that brief, but powerful eruption of feeling from the gut. It is the feeling of power, confidence, and satisfaction, all rolled into one.

The "winning feeling" feels good. And the same desire to taste that feeling stirs within every man to some extent. It's a desire passed up through his lineage from the dawning days of history, when his ancestors competed in the ultimate athletic contests of their day. Their opponents were wild beasts and fierce warriors. For them, defeat was death. Victory was life—reason enough to whoop and raise a clenched fist in the air.

Of course, winners in ultramodern arenas still raise their clenched fists into the air; while sportscasters sit on the sidelines and talk about life and death situations. They talk about teams and players and say things like, "It's all over." or "There's no tomorrow." But fortunately, defeat in the sport's world doesn't normally spell death. And there's always next season. But still, the mind and body of a man respond to a real challenge in only one way. Whether anticipating a battle to the death, or the game of the century, adrenalin finds its way into the blood stream, excites the body and prepares it for the moment of truth. On the edge of the confrontation there is always the pang of fear—losing always a possibility. There is the hunger for victory. Balanced between the equal possibilities is the keen sense of aliveness—every muscle engaged—every thought focused. Strength is felt here, weakness there—both mind and body tested. In the end there is pleasure or pain.

The pain is always there. It's always there in equal measure to balance the pleasure of winning. That's the

way the equation works. The ancient man defeated wild beasts or fierce warriors, and knew the ultimate pleasure of winning another day of life. In defeat he knew the ultimate pain—death. A champion athlete knows the pleasure of great sport's victories, but always, in the balance, is the equal measure of pain in defeat. If a winner wants to know great victories, he must be willing to risk suffering equally great defeats. Few are willing to take the risk. That's one reason 17,000 sit in the stands, while ten perform on the arena floor.

Millions do, however, participate in "their" sports every year. They pick up one sport or another and pit themselves against the task—the game, the distance, the weight. They test their mind and muscles. The run tightens their muscles. The golf game demands their concentration. But weekend athletes don't push their minds and bodies *too* far. They hold something back. They don't risk putting *all* of themselves into the effort. That way, losing doesn't mean as much. It isn't as painful. That's why the feelings that accompany the weekend athlete's winning and losing are so lukewarm. That's why, when he has finished exercising, he finds his place in the stands with the thousands of others who look to the true athletes to provide them with their minimum daily requirement of winning.

From a safe seat in the stands, the spectator can watch others risk the pain. He can watch the athlete risk the pain of pushing his body to its limits of speed, strength, and endurance. He can watch the player risk the pain of failing before the crowd—dropping the sure touchdown pass or missing the sure basket. He watches others struggle, and risk the pain of realizing the best of their efforts and talents aren't good enough—someone is better. And even though he may not realize it, he watches athletes risk the pain of knowing, on the edge of victory, that they are afraid of winning—afraid of the responsibility it will bring upon them to win again. But it's relatively painless for the spectator to sit and watch someone else who dares to give enough of himself to make the "winning" satisfying enough to go around.

The potential for physical and mental pain in sports is as real as the potential for the excitement of competing and the thrill of winning. That's why there are more spectators than sportsmen. The spectator can choose what he wants to feel. He can even switch teams in the middle of a game to guarantee he gets in on the "winning." The athlete, though, is committed to his team, his sport, himself. He can't give up on any of them. And it takes a degree of mental toughness—a special kind of courage—to withstand the pain, the adversity of sport. The commitment and the degree of toughness are the things that separate the weekender from the true athlete. But when the television screen shows a Reggie Jackson belt three home runs in the seventh game of a World Series; a Larry Bird issue a series of clutch passes and shots to help bring his Boston Celtic team another NBA crown; or a John Riggins bull through the NFL playoffs to set rushing records and carry the Washington Redskins to a Super Bowl win; it is clear there is another edge to the successful athlete—a winner's edge.

Doing The Job—*Not all of Larry's moves are pretty. He just does what it takes to win.*

Photo by Dick Raphael

In a way, an athlete is like a two-edge sword. He has one edge that is hard and blunt. It is this edge of his nature he uses to fend off the bad breaks, the physical insults to his body, and the many other adversities that would otherwise break his spirit. His other edge is as hard and durable. After all, it is made from the same alloy of character traits—the same mettle. But this other edge has been carefully honed to a sharpness that allows him to charge through to win, no matter how difficult the battle.

A winner's edge is what a champion like Larry Bird displays when he senses the time in the game when the contest will be won or lost. He is always there with his edge in the crucial moments of a game. He finds that extra burst of energy or makes the miracle play. He does whatever it takes to win the game. He has the edge.

And his edge is vision. Not 20/20 vision or court vision, but the champion has a clear vision of reality that gives him an edge. He knows what he can do and what he cannot. Such vision allows him to sort out the goals he can accomplish from the ones he can't. Then he sets his sights on the highest one he can reach. Of course, his vision also shows him how difficult the road he has chosen will be; but the same vision allows him to focus on his one most important goal to the point that he can't see anything else.

Larry Bird has such vision. He has been focused on basketball most of his life. The game has become his life. He has dedicated himself to becoming the best basketballl player in the world, because he can see that's what he can be. Vision is the edge.

His edge is talent. That is obvious. He is 6'9", 220 lbs. Larry Bird's long, lean frame, his heart that pumps twenty-five liters of blood a minute, and his respiratory system that gives him a maximal oxygen consumption capacity of fifty-five milliliters per kilogram, are what allow him to enjoy the success he has had in the NBA. His body fits the game, just as the powerful, compact body of Kurt Thomas fits gymnastics, and the spare, medium frame of Alberto Salazar fits long distance running.

But an equally important God-given talent of an athlete is the result of the organization of his brain and nervous system. Albert Einstein's brain and nervous system allowed him to analyze complex mathematical data and formulate universal theories. A great athlete's neurological organization allows him to analyze data on speed, direction, position, and formulate reactions in the form of passes, shots, swings of the bat, etc. That kind of natural talent allows Larry Bird to throw those look-one-way-throw-another passes. And his ability to see, analyze, and respond to what happens on the basketball court, along with his other physical talents, helps make the difference between winning and losing. Talent is his edge.

His edge is training. Natural talent goes unnoticed, unless harnessed to achieve a particular goal. That's why world class swimmers and gymnasts train four to six hours a day, six days a week, fifty-two weeks a year. It takes even gifted athletes that degree of strenuous

Photo by Poynter

Clutch Shooter—*When the Celtics need a key basket, they look to Bird. He's at his best when the pressure is on.*

training to master the unique set of precise muscle movements that belong to their sport. It takes the mind working with the muscles to learn those movements. And the learning comes only through repetition.

All world class athletes put in similar amounts of time and effort to master their sports. An athlete like Larry Bird realizes he wins or loses a game before he walks onto the floor. Practice is where he learns to perfectly execute every move he will use in the game. Practice,

Photo by Dick Raphael

Nothing Is Easy—*Every team in the NBA keys their defense on Bird. But he has such great determination and concentration, he still scores, rebounds, passes—contributes what his team needs for it to win.*

too, is where he makes his body ready for the demands of the sport. He realizes that winners win because they prepare to win. At the end of the 1980 NBA season, Larry showed that even a professional needs to prepare to win. As he left for summer vacation, he vowed to his teammates that he would work on his shooting, his passing, his running. He did. It was that next season the Celtics won their fourteenth title. Larry was ready. Training is his edge.

Winning is his edge. A basketball game has a beginning, an end, and a lot of uncharted territory between. Winning and losing are the two destinations at the end of the game. A team can take a number of paths from beginning to end, but always ends as a winner or loser. But once a team has gone from beginning to end and ended up a winner, it has a better idea of which turns to take to get there.

There are little things to be learned from winning games. Learning how much determination it takes to win is one. Learning how to react to the shifts in momentum is another. It's possible the ability to sense the very moment when a great effort will win the game can be learned, too. But what it boils down to is that when a player has done something once, it's easier for him to do it again.

Larry Bird knows the way to winning like the back of his hand. He has been there many times in high school, college, and the pros. He likes it there. He never gets tired of that trip. Winning is his edge.

Losing is his edge. Even though losing isn't the chosen destination, even champions end up there. Larry Bird loses approximately twenty games a year with the Celtics. But he wins sixty. He turns losing into a lesson that helps him earn those wins.

Of course, the first thing he does after a defeat is feel the pain and disappointment. But later, in the quiet of the locker room or on the plane ride back to Boston, he looks back at the game with his mind's eye and looks for his faults. He asks himself if he shot the ball too much, or not enough. He asks himself if he was in good enough shape, or did his legs give out in the final quarter. He asks himself if the team worked together, or could he have said or done something to help it work better. He asks himself if he wanted to win badly enough.

A champion faces defeat. But in defeat, he takes a hard look at himself. He looks for the things he can improve. He works to improve himself. He walks onto the floor a better player the next game. Losing is his edge.

A champion has vision, knows talent, knows how to prepare to win, knows how to win, and knows how to lose. He takes the risk of sport. He earns the reward of great victories. He becomes a hero, a celebrity of the crowd, because he produces that "winning feeling." He may be paid a million dollars a year to do it.

But the lasting gift of the champion isn't what he does, but that he does. Records are broken, Statistics are forgotten. He may be remembered as a great football, basketball, or baseball player; but more important, a champion, like Larry Bird, should be remembered as a man who dared to show others how to win.

To me, a winner is someone who recognizes his God-given talents, works his tail off to develop them into skills, and uses those skills to accomplish his goals.

That's why a winner doesn't concentrate on beating an opponent; he concentrates on performing to the limit of his potential. That's why a winner doesn't just want to win; he wants to do whatever he must to prepare himself physically and mentally to win. That's why a winner doesn't think much about past victories or defeats; he focuses his thoughts on winning the next game. And that's why a winner doesn't just hope to win; he knows he will win.

I consider myself a winner. Not so much because I have been successful in the NBA, but because I have learned how to win. Sure, my God-given talents gave me the potential to become a top player in the NBA; but I wouldn't have reached that potential if I hadn't understood the keys to winning.

I first began to understand those keys while I was playing high school "ball." When I made the team, I made the decision to be the best player on our team. I was honest with myself. *I realized what my talents were.* I knew I was big for my age, and that I had a feel for the game. I knew I had the talent to be the best player on our team. *I locked my sights on that goal and didn't give up until I reached it.* I practiced the fundamentals of the game. I worked on weights and ran. *I did whatever I could to prepare myself to be the best basketball player I could be.* And then, I scrimmaged against my teammates. I played against other schools' players in games. Sometimes my team would win. And every time it did, I would understand better what kinds of things I had to do on the court to help my team win. *I learned how to win by winning.* Of course, my team didn't always win. And when it didn't, I would look back and see that if I had played a little better defense my man wouldn't have scored so many points, or that if I had rebounded better, our team might have controlled the "boards." *When I lost, I learned what my weaknesses were, and went out the next day to turn those weaknesses into strengths.*

I became the best player on our team. I helped my team enjoy a winning season. Then I set my sights on making a college team. And I did that. I kept setting my goals, and kept reaching them because I was always honest with myself, and knew I had the talent to achieve my goal. I knew I would have to prepare myself, and that I would win and lose before I reached my goal. But I knew I would reach it.

Your talent may not allow you to set your sights on a starting position in the NBA. The odds are against it. Last year only thirty-five basketball players in the entire country made it to the NBA. But basketball really wasn't meant to be a profession. It was meant to be fun. It was meant to be good exercise. And it was meant to be a good place to learn how to win.

You may only play basketball at the high school level. But, if you can truly say that you became the very best basketball player that your God-given talent would allow, you have accomplished as much as an NBA superstar. You have performed to the limit of your potential. And that's what a winner is all about.

PREPARE YOURSELF TO BE A WINNER

If you want to be a winner, you must prepare your mind and body to play like one. Every player, every team wants to win. But it is only the winner who makes ready his mind and body for the quick thinking and physical effort it takes to win basketball games. Below you will find ten suggestions to help you physically and mentally prepare to be a winner.

PHYSICAL CONDITIONING

☑ Check Your Diet

Your body is a biological machine. Its fuel is food. If you eat the right foods, your body-machine will run smoothly and efficiently. If not, it won't get the nutrients it needs, and won't perform at full speed or power.

It doesn't take a genius to understand that. And it doesn't take one to learn to eat right. You don't need to buy all your food at a health food store, swallow a handful of vitamins every day, or down several glasses of protein supplement to obtain the necessary vitamins, minerals, carbohydrates, fats, proteins, and water your body needs to function properly.

All you need to do to insure your body gets what it needs, is to select your daily menu from the United States Department of Agriculture's Basic Four Food Groups. This may sound old fashioned, but there is no scientific proof that a large intake of vitamins or protein improves athletic performance. If you select a variety of foods from the food groups shown below, you will provide your body with what it needs.

MILK GROUP (Select at least two servings a day from this group)

FOODS	NUTRIENT FORM	MINERALS	VITAMINS
Whole and Skimmed Milk Cottage Cheese Yogurt Ice Cream Cheese	Protein*	Calcium Phosphorus	A,C,D, Thiamine Riboflavin, Niacin

MEAT GROUP (Select two servings a day from this group)

FOODS	NUTRIENT FORM	MINERALS	VITAMINS
Beef Fish Veal Poultry Pork Eggs Liver Beans Heart Nuts Kidney Lentils	Protein* Some Fats* Little Carbohydrate*	Iron	A,C,D, Thiamine, Riboflavin, Niacin

FRUITS AND VEGETABLES (Select four or more servings a day from this group)

FOODS	NUTRIENT FORM	MINERALS	VITAMINS
Green and Yellow Fruits and Vegetables	Carbohydrates*	Iron Calcium Magnesium	A,C, Riboflavin

Fresh fruits and vegetables are a very important vitamin and mineral source. You should eat a dark green vegetable like spinach, broccoli, and kale, or a deep yellow vegetable like carrots, sweet potatoes, squash, and pumpkin every day.

BREAD AND CEREAL GROUP (Select four servings a day from this group)

FOODS	NUTRIENT FORM	MINERALS	VITAMINS

Enriched and Whole
  Grain Breads
Enriched and Whole
  Grain Cereals
	Carbohydrate*
	Some Protein*
		Calcium
		Iron
		Magnesium
			A,C, Riboflavin

*Proteins, fats, and carbohydrates are energy sources for the body. Carbohydrates are the body's favorite energy source, and approximately 60% of your diet should consist of carbohydrates. The best sources for carbohydrates are enriched breads, and fruits and vegetables.

Nonessential Foods

The fuel provided by the foods in the basic four groups provides your body with fuel and nutrients your body needs to build and repair itself. Other foods like candy, cokes, butter and margarine, and other snack foods provide energy only, and when not immediately needed are stored as fat.

As long as you have selected your menu from the Basic Four food groups, there is nothing wrong with occasionally eating from this group. But limit your consumption of these foods.

In addition to eating right, you should always eat your pregame or prepractice meal four hours before you play. This will insure that your food is digested and that you will have more body energy at your disposal to play basketball.

Your pregame meal should be selected from the Basic four food groups. There are no foods that will give you quick energy or extra strength. It takes hours or days for any food to be converted to a form that the body can use as energy.

Finally, along with eating right, you should drink plenty of water. Whenever you practice or play in a game, you should drink water when you feel thirsty. Water has many functions in the body. A lack of water can cause your body to overheat, cause you to fatigue quicker, and even cause you to become mentally confused.

Eat and drink right, and make sure your body gets what it needs.

☑ Check Your Strength

Common sense will tell you that the stronger your muscles, the better you will be able to perform as an athlete. The muscles do the work of the body, and if they are strong they can do more work and do it easier.

Of course, basketball players don't need to build large, massive muscles like body builders, but they do need to build their overall body strength. Good overall body strength makes it easier to play defense, rebound, and perform the other skills of the game.

In the preseason, I work out on Nautilus exercise machines. I have found that these machines provide the safest, most efficient way to build overall body strength. The Nautilus program enables me to exercise all the major muscle groups in three half hour sessions each week. Over a six month period it is possible to double the body's muscle strength in only three high intensity workouts per week.

There are other weight training programs you can use to build your body strength. I think Nautilus is the best and safest. The people at the Nautilus fitness center will help you set up an exercise program, and supervise your sessions. If there is no fitness center near you, have your coach help you set up a strength training program.

☑ Cardiovascular Conditioning

Basketball is a game played on the run. Along with building your overall body strength, you must condition your heart and vascular system to meet the body's demand for blood throughout a run-and-gun ball game.

The best exercise to condition the heart-vascular system is running. If you plan to put together a strength training and cardiovascular conditioning program, you should begin your strength training first. If you begin your strength training in June, for example, you would begin your running program in late July or early August.

The Nautilus workouts will strengthen your legs more than running, plus they will improve your cardiovascular conditioning to an extent. Both these gains will improve your running ability. So when you begin your running program, you will be able to concentrate on building your wind and endurance.

You should use the two months before you begin your running program to play ball, and work on fundamentals.

Photo by Poynter

EIGHT WEEK RUNNING PROGRAM

1st WEEK—	Tuesday	Jog** 1½ miles; cool down****—walk ¼ mile.	
	Thursday	Jog 1½ miles; cool down—walk ¼ mile.	
	Saturday	Jog 1 mile; run*** 1 mile (time your run); cool down—walk ¼ mile.	
2nd WEEK—	Tuesday	Jog 1½ miles; cool down—walk ¼ mile.	
	Thursday	Run 1½ miles (try for six minute mile pace or better); sprint 50 yds four times; cool down—walk ¼ mile.	
	Saturday	Jog 1 mile; run 1½ miles; cool down—walk ¼ mile.	
3rd WEEK—	Tuesday	Run 1½ miles; sprint 50 yards four times; cool down—walk ¼ mile.	
	Thursday	Run 1½ miles; sprint 50 yards four times; cool down—walk ¼ mile.	
	Saturday	Jog 1 mile; run 2 miles (six minute mile pace); cool down—walk ¼ mile.	
4th WEEK—	Tuesday	Run 2 miles; sprint 50 yards four times; cool down—walk ¼ mile.	
	Thursday	Run 1½ miles; sprint 50 yards six times; cool down—walk ¼ mile.	
	Saturday	Run 3 miles; cool down—walk ¼ mile.	
5th WEEK—	Tuesday	Run 2 miles; sprint 50 yards six times; cool down—walk ¼ mile.	
	Thursday	Run 2 miles; sprint 50 yards six times; cool down—walk ¼ mile.	
	Saturday	Run 3½ miles; cool down—walk ¼ mile.	
6th WEEK—	Tuesday	Run 2½ miles; sprint 50 yards six times; cool down—walk ¼ mile.	
	Thursday	Run 2½ miles; run 50 yards six times; cool down—walk ¼ mile.	
	Saturday	Run 4 miles; cool down—walk ¼ mile.	
7th WEEK—	Tuesday	Run 3 miles; sprint 50 yards six times; cool down—walk ¼ mile.	
	Thursday	Run 3 miles; sprint 50 yards six times; cool down—walk ¼ mile.	
	Saturday	Run 4.5 miles; cool down—walk ¼ mile.	
8th WEEK—	Tuesday	Run 3.5 miles; sprint 50 yards six times; cool down—walk ¼ mile.	
	Thursday	Run 3 miles; sprint 50 yards six times; cool down—walk ¼ mile.	
	Saturday	Run 5 miles; cool down—walk ¼ mile.	

(WARM UP marked vertically along left of workout column; COOL DOWN**** marked vertically along right.)*

**Warmup—See following section on flexibility.

**Jog—A slow, relaxed running pace.

***Run—Every time you run try to achieve a six minute mile pace.

****Cool Down—Walk at the end of your running exercises.
Do this so your heart rate will slow more gradually, and your blood will again evenly distribute throughout your body.

You should always check with your doctor before beginning a running program.

You should also check with him if you ever feel pain in your head, neck, shoulder, arm, chest (a feeling like someone is sitting on your chest).

☑ Check Your Flexibility

You are able to shoot, dribble, and move on the basketball court, because your skeletal muscles pull on your bones and make them move. Your muscles are able to pull your bones this way and that because your arms and legs are made up of several bones connected by ball-and-socket-like joints at the shoulder, hip and elbow, and by more hinge-like joints at the knee, wrist, and ankle. Tough bands of tissue called ligaments connect the bones at these points. Tough cord-like tissues connect the muscles to the bones and muscles to other muscles.

During physical exercise, the muscle, ligament, tendon units that make movement possible are put under stress. The more flexible the connective and muscle tissues are, the less likely it will be for those tissues to pull or tear.

As you can see from the pictures on this and other pages, all of the Celtics go through a series of stretching exercises before every game and practice session. These exercises increase the flexibility of muscles, ligaments, and tendons. They also temporarily gorge the stretched muscle with blood which warms its tissues, thus preparing it for strenuous exercise. Also such stretching exercises stimulate the production of fluid that lubricates the joints. You should also use these exercises at the end of strenuous exercise. They will decrease muscle soreness.

Learn the proper stretching exercises for your sport, and use them before you play or practice. Remember, though, your muscles, tendons, and ligaments are not rubber bands. You must move into a particular muscle stretching position slowly. And once you are in a position, hold it for between forty and fifty seconds. If your muscles are extremely tight, you may want to go through the set of stretching exercises one time, and hold each position twenty seconds. Then, go through the set of exercises a second time and hold each position thirty seconds.

Stretching exercises will increase your flexibility. Increased flexibility will not only improve your ability to perform, but also decrease the chance of injury. Improving your flexibility through stretching exercises is another way to prepare yourself to win.

☑ Check the Skills You Need to Practice

Basketball players must master all the skills of their game. They can't, like the football quarterback or lineman, specialize and concentrate on a few of their game's skills.

If you want to be a top basketball player, you must learn each of the game's basic skills, its fundamentals. Learning those fundamentals requires understanding and repetition.

You learn skills, like dribbling, like this: you watch your coach demonstrate dribbling; you try to imitate the muscle movements your coach made; you make those movements over and over until you feel comfortable making them—until you have learned to dribble.

What happens is that you see your coach, the way his body is positioned, and how his hand and wrist move to dribble the ball. Your brain takes in that information, and then sends weak electrical messages down nerves that are attached to your muscles. The messages tell your muscles how much and when to contract or relax, so that your arm dribbles the ball.

Bischoff Photo

***Warmup**—I use stretching exercises to prepare my body for strenuous exercise.*

The problem is that the muscles have never worked together quite that way before. They try, but they can't quite get it together. That's why you feel awkward when you try to do something for the first time. The muscles feel awkward, too, and send messages back to the brain to tell it what they did. They let the brain know what mistakes they made, so that it can send the muscles new instructions that will help them perform next time they're asked to dribble. So when you want to try to dribble again, the brain gives the muscles a better set of instructions. The muscles contract or relax, you dribble, and your muscles again talk to your brain to let it know how they're doing. When the message from the muscles to the brain says "We're doing it just like you ask." you have learned to dribble. From then on, the brain sends its prerecorded message when you want to dribble, and the muscles do their thing.

Because of the way you learn, one of the most important things you can do is find a good teacher. Your teacher may be a coach, a parent, a book on basketball fundamentals, or a star player whose moves you watch and study. No matter who or what your teacher is, make sure you completely understand what you're supposed to do before you try to do it. The better picture you have of what you're supposed to do, the better you can learn to do it.

Another thing to remember is that you will never be too good to practice. Once you have practiced enough to learn the fundamentals, you will need to practice to refine your skills to the point that you can execute them without thinking. Once you have refined your basic skills, you will need to practice putting your skills together in effective combinations, like putting your shooting and dribbling together with fakes and moves to the basket. Once you have practiced enough to combine skills, you will need to practice to add skills to your game, like the ability to shoot with one hand as well as with the other. You will always have weak points to make strong, and strong points to make stronger.

Practice is a part of the game. As long as you play basketball, you will practice basketball. And when you do practice, execute every skill, every move the same way you expect to in the game. Fake the way you will fake; drive to the basket with the same speed and power as you will in a game. You will play the way you practice, so practice fundamental basketball, practice using all your concentration, practice using all the physical and mental talents you've got. Practice being a winner.

Bischoff Photo

MENTAL CONDITIONING

☑ Check Your Diet

Just as you should eat the right foods so your body will function at its peak efficiency, you must feed your mind the right foods so it will function at its best, too. Of course, information is the food of the mind.

First, you need to feed your mind the kind of information it needs to help it learn the basketball fundamentals. In the section above on skills practice, you saw how the brain and muscles communicate information back and forth through the nerves until a skill is learned. From that knowledge, you should see how important it is to feed your mind vivid pictures and descriptions of the skill you want to learn. If you want to learn to dribble the ball, for example, you should read books that describe dribbling, study photographs and illustrations of players dribbling, and watch how star players dribble. There is actually scientific proof to show that when you watch someone perform a physical skill, like dribbling, and concentrate on the dribbling motion, your brain, without you being conscious of it, sends very weak messages to your muscles through the nerves. These message aren't strong enough to make the muscles work, but they are strong enough that the muscles learn something about the skill from the vivid pictures you fed your mind.

The second type of information you need to feed your mind is that which it uses to energize your body. All players experience games in which they're "up" for the contest. Everything they do seems to go right, and they work hard, but don't get tired. Likewise, all players experience games in which they're "flat." Nothing seems to go right, and they don't have energy to hustle. They get tired at the end of the game. Players can get the same amount of sleep, go through the same practice sessions before a contest, but when they walk onto the floor, they may be "up" for the game, go "flat," or perform somewhere between the two.

Coaches feel it is their job to get their players mentally prepared for a game. They all use different methods. They all feed their players different information to motivate them. Some try to "psyche up" their players with pep talks. They talk about school pride, doing one's best for the team, and things like that. Some coaches get their players fired up and mad at the other team. Some will tell their players how good they are. Others will tell them how bad they are, and that faces on the starting lineup will change if things don't change. Every coach uses different sets of information to motivate players to play to their potential.

The problem is that a coach can use every trick in the book, but his players will still go out onto the floor, and some will be "up" for the game, some will go "flat," and others will play somewhere between. The reason is that every player is motivated by different feelings. Some players can be motivated by pep talks. Some can't. Some players don't play their best unless they are sick to their stomach before a game. Some players have to work themselves up to be mad at the other team before they give the game all they've got. Another player will play best if he's afraid he'll lose his starting position. The

same fear may cause another player to tighten up and play poorly. Every player has a unique set of thoughts and feelings that motivate him, and unlock the potential energy.

I'm sure you have played in a regulation or sandlot game in which you seemed to flow with the game. Your shots went in; you always seemed to make the right play; you played at full speed and never got tired. That is the feeling you want to have in every game. But to unlock the energy that allows you to play that way, you must find the emotional key to unlock it. Did you play your best when you were mad before the game, or when you were so nervous that you were sick to your stomach? Did you just feel relaxed? If you can determine what set of feelings unlocks your energy, you can feed your mind the kind of information that will make you feel those feelings.

I play my best when I feel confident about the game. I don't mean the kind of confidence some players show when they boast they're going to win this or that game, and don't really believe it. That's false confidence. The kind of confidence I'm talking about is the kind I feel when I know I have done everything I can to prepare for the game, that I believe in the abilities of my teammates, and that I trust and respect the judgement of my coaches. When I feel the confidence of knowing those things, I don't care what team we're going to play. I know that the team and I are going out on the floor and play to the best of our potential. And that's enough to get me "psyched" for a game.

Because I know what feeling motivates me, I sit in the locker room before a game and feed my mind with information that makes me feel confident. I think about how hard I've worked in practice; I think of the games in which our team worked together and pulled out a big win; I think of some of the key changes our coach made that won games for us in the past. I roll those things over in my mind. I feel confident. I walk out on the floor, quietly and confidently. I play my game full blast.

Learn what thoughts best prepare you mentally for a game. Think like a winner.

☑ Check Your Strength

The basketball player's mind must be as strong as his body. He must be mentally tough so he can keep a clear head throughout the contest and make the split-second decisions he must during the game. This is difficult, because of the many things which happen during a basketball game which can destroy his concentration. Opponents do whatever they can to shake his confidence and break his concentration. The opponents' cheer leaders and fans do the same with their shouts and yells. His own coach may yell at him. The referee blows the whistle at him. And there will be times when nothing goes right, and his team is behind by twenty points with just a few minutes to play. There are a lot of excuses for a player to give up.

If you want to be a top player, you must learn to ignore the game's distractions and concentrate on one thing— playing basketball. If you can do that, you won't even hear the crowd. You will be able to play with as much ease and confidence as you do in a sandlot game. But learning to concentrate is the most difficult thing you can do. Few people can concentrate on one thing for more than thirty seconds. How long can you read this book without flipping through the pages to look at the pictures? Probably not long. Like everyone else, you need to develop your ability to concentrate. You need to build your mental toughness.

Here is an exercise that will help you improve your concentration: every day, find a spot in your home or at school where you can sit quietly and uninterrupted for about half an hour. Your room at home would be a very good place, so pretend you're there.

You can sit or lay down. Once you are in position, close your eyes and relax. Just sit there for about a minute and think about anything you want. After about a minute, start thinking about the neighborhood or subdivision in which your home is located. In your mind see your neighbors houses, the roads, the streets, the trees. After you can see your neighborhood clearly, move down the road your house is on and see the houses along the way. Move down the road until you come to your driveway. Go down your driveway and look at your house. Start with the front of it and study the front wall and see its doors, windows, and anything else you can see—the paint, the brick, etc. Move around the house and study all the walls. When you come back around to the front of the house, go in the front door and walk through the house into your room. Once inside, with your eyes still closed, use your mind to look around and see everything you can identify on the walls of your room. Once you have gone all around the room, use your mind's eye to see yourself. Look at yourself, the way your hair is combed, the way you are dressed. Finally, once you have studied yourself, still, with your mind, concentrate on your belt buckle, or a button on your shirt. See the button, for instance, in as much detail as you can. Run your mind over it again and again. See its color and texture, the way the thread comes up through it. If you can focus your thoughts on that button without thinking about anything else, you are concentrating.

When you begin, you will only be able to concentrate on the button for a few seconds or minutes. If you work at it every day, though, you can build your concentration just as you can build the strength in your arms by gradually adding more weight to a barbell. When you can concentrate on one thing for between thirty and sixty minutes, you're pretty strong.

Another way you can build your mental strength is to build your confidence. Confidence, like concentration is another mind muscle you can flex.

One step you can take to build your confidence is to establish a preseason training program. You can set up a running and strength conditioning program as discussed under physical conditioning. If you can set strength and endurance goals for yourself, and reach them before the season starts, you can be confident that you are ready for the basketball season.

Once the season has begun, you can set other goals for yourself. You can set the goal of increasing the num-

No Time To Rest—*I rest my body on the bench, but not my mind. I concentrate on every play as if I were out on the floor playing in the game. I am mentally prepared to get into the flow of the game whenever the coach sends me back onto the court.*

Photo by Dick Raphael

ber of free throws you can sink out of a given number of attempts. You can set the goal of improving your ability to shoot with your "off" hand. When you set and achieve goals like these, you build confidence in your ability to play the game, little by little.

You can additionally build your confidence by establishing good working relationships with your teammates and coaches. For instance, you can communicate with your teammates, so that they know how they can help you, and you know how to help them. You may tell a teammate that you know he likes to take shots from the deep corner, and that you will pick or screen his man to help him get free for those shots. At the same time you can mention to your teammate the areas on the court from which you like to shoot, so he will know to pick for you or look to pass the ball to you in those areas.

You should also communicate with your coaches to make sure you know what they expect from you. Ask what role they expect you to play. When you know your role, and understand how your teammates and coaches contribute to the team effort, you can be confident.

Once the game starts, you will use your concentration to keep your mind on what you need to do to win. And you will be sure you can do what it takes to win if you have taken the steps to build your confidence. Concentration and confidence are two mind muscles winners flex. Develop them so you are mentally tough enough to be a winner.

☑ Check Your "Cardiovascular" Conditioning

In the section on physical conditioning, I outlined a running program to help you condition your heart and vascular system for running up and down the court. But basketball players have another kind of heart within them, too. But it's a kind of heart that all the running in the world won't condition.

The kind of heart I'm talking about is the one that keeps a player trying his flat out best every minute he's on the court. It's that force inside that makes him dive to the floor for a loose ball. It's the something special within that drives him to give his best even when he's sick or injured. It's the "heart" that allows him to run up and down the court and give his best, no matter what the score, until the final buzzer sounds.

Some payers are born with such a strong "heart." They naturally give the game, or anything else they do, all their effort. But while others may have some desire to play the game, their heart is too weak to allow them to give that little extra effort that means the difference between the great player and the average player, and winning and losing.

Many players never develop the kind of heart I'm talking about. They are like most people. They don't give their best to anything because they don't really understand what they're trying to accomplish. For instance, students will read books, listen to lectures, and take tests, but they won't give school their best effort. Because they don't understand that their effort in the classroom determines what kind of job they will get, the kind of house they will live in, and the kind of things they will do the rest of their lives. Likewise, basketball players don't understand what giving their best to a game can mean to them.

Basketball is fun. It's good exercise. But it's also a classroom where you can learn to set and achieve goals, learn your physical and mental strengths and weaknesses, how to work as a member of a team, and how to hang in there when things get tough—a lot of things that can help you the rest of your life. And the more effort you put into the game, the more self knowledge, fun, and exercise you will get out of it.

But remember, if you decide to give 100 percent of yourself to a basketball game, you'll need to condition your "heart" for the effort. A marathon runner doesn't just start out running twenty-six miles, 385 yards. He begins by running a fraction of that distance. He runs, strengthens his cardiovascular system, and builds his endurance. Then he adds another mile, then another, until he can cover the distance. And once he can cover it, he further conditions himself to cover it as fast as he can.

Giving 100 percent of your effort from beginning to end of a basketball game is similar to running a given distance. Of course, the distance covered is time. And the "heart" you need to cover the distance with your best effort doesn't pump blood throughout the body. It's the one down deep that pushes you to do your best. And if you're not accustomed to giving your best, you'll quickly find out what kind of shape your "heart" is in.

Let's say you start by covering a short distance. Concentrate on one phase of the game, say defense. For a quarter, or a given number of minutes in a game, see if you can use every ounce of your talent and energy to play the toughest defense you can play on your man. Now, when you do this, you're going to have to be honest with yourself. Because you are the only one who can know if you give your best. And you'll know because it will hurt, especially if you've never done it. After a few minutes of concentrated effort, the force inside that drives you will weaken. No longer will you be giving your best. You'll slack off because your "heart" isn't in shape to go the distance.

But keep at it. Set goals you can reach. Gradually increase the time you can give your best effort. Eventually you'll be able to give 100 percent every minute of the game. You'll be known as one of those players who play with a lot of "heart."

Showing Some "Heart"—*I give my best on every play. That's my responsibility to my team, the fans, and myself.*

Photo by Dick Raphael

☑ Check Your Flexibility

When a big game is about to start, and the fans are going wild, it's hard for a player to stay relaxed. Thoughts about winning, losing, and whether or not he's going to have a good game run through his mind. The game will challenge him. And his natural reaction to a challenge is a pounding heart and tense muscles. But if a player tenses his muscles too much, he's going to walk out onto the floor and "choke" in the big game.

You have probably heard someone talk about a player or team "choking" in a crucial game. It may have been a championship game that a team wanted to win badly. It may have been when time was running out, and a player had a chance to win the game with an easy shot. Whatever the situations, the "choking" took place because the player was so "tight" that his performance was affected.

Players "choke" when they think or worry too much about a game. Their mind focuses on their weaknesses, the strength of their opponents, or the possibility of losing. And when the mind locks into thinking about those things, it causes the body to prepare for a threatening situation and tense its muscles. When all the muscles are tensed, the body won't move smoothly and easily—the way it must to execute basketball skills.

If you bend your arm at the elbow, you can see why a body of tensed muscles won't work smoothly. As you bring your arm toward you, you can feel that the muscles on the inside of your arm contract, while the muscles on the outside of your arm relax. Other parts of your body move one way or another because one set of muscles contract while another set relax. So, you can see that if both sets are tensed, one set of muscles must relax more or one must contract more if a particular part of the body is to move. When it does move, the arm or leg motion is herky-jerky. That's why players don't perform well when they're too nervous.

"Clutch" players, players who perform best in pressure situations, do so because they have great mental flexibility. They worry about the game, but they do their worrying before the game starts. And they don't just worry. They think of all the things they need to do to prepare themselves for the big game. So when it's time for the big game, they may be a little nervous, but they don't waste time thinking about how important the game is, or whether or not they're going to make a mistake. They've already done their worrying and preparation. When the game starts, they quit thinking. They just open up their mind so it can work on the game.

You, too, can maintain your mental flexibility by thinking about what you need to think about when you need to think about it. When you know a big game is coming up, work on the weak points of your game. That's the time to worry and do something about the weaknesses that may cause you to lose. When it's time for the game, it's time to stop worrying and preparing. It's time to play. And it's time for your mind to be ready like your muscles—slightly tensed so you are alert, but not too locked in on one thought or another, so that you are ready to react to any situation.

And when your mind muscle is only slightly tensed, you will be able to anticipate action on the court better. If you're not focusing your mind on passing the ball to a particular place, or shooting the ball from a particular spot, your mind will be able to react quicker when it realizes a man is open for a pass or that you are open for a shot. You won't force the action. You will react to it. Your mind will be flexibile and react to whatever happens. For instance, when the momentum of a game shifts against your team, you will be able to realize your team is going through a tough stretch. You won't worry about it. You won't try to force shots or passes. You will dig in and focus your mind on holding on until the momentum shifts. And when you see a break, a steal or a blocked shot that turns into a fast break and two points, you can shift gears. When the momentum shifts your way, you will be ready to react and ride it like a wave as far is it will take you.

Use your mind to think about what you need to think about when you need to think about it. Keep your mind relaxed and ready, and your muscles will be too.

☑ Check The Skills You Need To Practice

In the explanation of other preparation tips, I explained that the more vividly you can visualize the skill you were trying to learn, the quicker and easier you can learn it. Also, I explained an exercise you can use to improve your concentration. Now, I'm going to have you put together the visualizing of how skills should be performed with the concentration exercise, so you can learn to practice basketball skills in your head.

Here is how to do it: at the end of your concentration exercises (described under the heading "Check your strength"), visualize a fundamental you want to practice, for example, shooting. See yourself going up for a jump shot with perfect form. Feel yourself taking the ball up with an easy, fluid motion. See and hear the ball swish through the net.

I used this practice technique when I realized I wasn't concentrating on the ball when I went up to block shots. I was just sticking my hand up in the vicinity of the ball and hoping to block it. So in my mental practice session, I would visualize myself going up to block a shot. I would see the shooter raise the ball into shooting position, and would keep my eye on the ball until I saw my hand knock it away. Then I would watch my hands try to grab the ball. After a few mental practice sessions, I began keeping my eye on the ball when I went up to block shots in a game.

A mental workout is not only a good way to work on your weak points, but also a good way to prepare for a game. Always go through a mental rehearsal before a game. Go through your concentration exercise first. Then visualize and feel yourself shooting, dribbling, rebounding, etc. See yourself executing all aspects of your game perfectly. Hear the crowd roaring for you. Practice being a winner.

GLOSSARY

Air Ball—A shot that completely misses the backboard and rim.

Alley-Oop—A well timed pass-shot combination usually executed by a guard and a forward. It is initiated when a guard makes a lob pass which leads the forward to the basket in such a way that he needs only to move to the basket, jump up and guide the ball into the basket.

Anticipation—The ability to sense the next move of a teammate or an opponent before he makes it.

Arc—The trajectory of the ball in flight.

Assist—A pass from one player to another which results in the pass receiver scoring a basket.

Backboard—(glass, board, bankboard) The rectangular surface perpendicular to the court and to which the basket is attached.

Backdoor—A situation in which an offensive man without the ball cuts behind his defender to the basket to receive a pass.

Bank Shot—A shot made by bouncing the ball off a particular spot on the backboard so it caroms off into the basket.

Blocking—An illegal movement of a defensive player into the path of an offensive player in such a way that he interferes with the offensive man's free movement.

Bomb—A shot taken from long range.

Bonus—An extra shot given a free-throw shooter if he sinks the first free throw awarded for a one-shot foul.

Box Out—Same as blocking out—the act of positioning your body between an opponent and a rebound.

Bucket—(hoop, basket, two points) A field goal.

Center—(Pivotman, bigman, man-in-the-middle) A forward who plays the center area of the court.

Center Circle—The four-foot circle in the middle of the court which is divided down the middle by the midcourt line.

Center Jump—The opening play of each game in which the two opposing centers stand facing each other on either side of the midcourt line, inside either half of the center circle. The referee tosses the ball into the air, and both centers attempt to tip the ball to one of their teammates.

Change of Pace—The act of an offensive player alternately speeding up and slowing down in an attempt to throw his defender off balance, so he is freed for a shot or can drive around his defender to the basket.

Charging—A personal foul committed when an offensive player runs into a defensive player who has established his position on the court. The defensive player has the right to position his body in the path of an offensive player, but he must reach his spot on the floor and set his feet facing the offensive man before the offensive man collides with him, or the defensive man will be called for blocking.

Charity Line—The free-throw line.

Cheap Basket—(Garbage shot) An easy scoring shot near the basket; the result of poor defense rather than good offense.

Clear-the-Boards—(Crashing-the-boards) Grabbing a rebound.

Cold—(Cold streak, off-night) The temporary inability of a shooter to hit shots he would normally hit.

Cross Court Pass—A pass thrown laterally, from one sideline to another. It is generally considered an easy pass to intercept, because it must either be thrown through or lobbed over the defense.

Crossover—A change of direction step used by offensive players in which one foot crosses over the other.

Division Line—(Timeline) The midcourt line.

Double Figures—Term used to state that a player has scored more than nine points.

Double Dribble—The name of the violation committed when a dribbler starts his dribble, stops it, and then starts it again. When his violation is committed, the referee will award possession of the ball to the defensive team.

Double Team—The guarding of one offensive player by two defenders.

Downcourt—The end of the court opposite the one in which play is taking place.

Downtown—A long range shot.

Draw the Foul—This is what an offensive player does when he deliberately moves in such a way as to cause an opponent to foul him.

Dribble—Bouncing the ball on the floor and controlling it with hand, arm, and wrist motion.

Drive—The act of an offensive player moving quickly to the basket with the ball in a scoring attempt.

Dunk—(Stuff, Jam) A shot made with one or two hands by leaping high in the air and dropping or throwing the ball over the rim and into the basket.

Endline—The line at the end of the court that runs the width of the playing area and joins the two sidelines.

Fadeaway Jumper—A jump shot taken as the shooter's body falls away from the basket.

Fast Break—The quick movement of the ball downcourt by a team that has gained possession of the ball by grabbing a defensive rebound.

Feed—Passing the ball to a player who is in good shooting position.

Field Goal—(Hoop, bucket, basket) Two points made by sinking a shot from the field.

Field Goal Percentage—A calculation made by dividing the number of field goals made by the number of shots taken and multiplying by one hundred.

Fingertip Control—The ability to control the ball by using the fingertips instead of the palms of the hands.

Follow Through—The continuation of a player's hand and body motion even after he has released the shot or pass.

Follow Up—The act of a shooter quickly moving to the basket to get in rebound position for the shot he has just taken. It is also the act of quickly putting up another shot off a rebound.

Forcing the Shot—Shooting the ball when well-defended, or shooting a shot that shouldn't have been taken.

Forecourt—The portion of the court nearest the offensive team's basket.

Forwards—The two players who play in the frontcourt on either side of the center.

Foul Out—To use up the allowed number of fouls and be forced to leave the game. In high school and college basketball five fouls are allowed, in pro ball six.

Free Throw Line—The line parallel to the endline and fifteen feet in front of the backboard. It is the twelve-foot line behind which players must stand when shooting free throws.

Free Throw Line—The line parallel to the endline and fifteen feet in front of the backboard. It is the twelve foot line behind which players must stand behind when shooting free-throws.

Free Throw Percentage—The calculation made by dividing the number of free throws made by the number taken and multiplying by one hundred.

Freeze—The term used when a team leading a game attempts to run out the clock by maintaining possession of the ball.

Front or Fronting—The act of a defensive player denying the offensive player the ball by establishing defensive position between his man and the ball.

Frontcourt—The end of the court which contains the offensive team's goal.

Give-and-Go—The offensive play executed when a player with the ball passes to another player, then cuts to the basket to receive a return pass.

Goal—(Hoop, bucket, basket, field goal) Two points made by sinking a shot from the field.

Goal Tending—The violation committed when a player interferes with a shot after it begins its downward motion to the basket, or when it is within the basket or the imaginary cylinder that extends upward from the ring of the rim.

Go Baseline— A phrase used to describe the move of an offensive player to the basket on a path between his defender and the baseline.

Guards—The two backcourt positions played by players adept at ball handling and dribbling.

Gun or Gunner—A player who shoots the ball every time he gets a chance.

Hack or Hacking—A foul committed when a defender slaps or hits an offensive player.

Held Ball—The situation existing when two or more opposing players have their hands on the ball so that no player can gain possession of the ball without undue force.

Helping Out—To help a teammate guard his man.

Hook Shot—A shot executed by beginning with your back to the basket and delivered by extending your arm out from the body with the ball laying in the hand and moving the ball toward the basket in an arc-like motion.

Hoop—The goal or basket, or the act of scoring a goal or basket.

Hot Hand—The term used when a player hits most of the shots he puts up.

Inbounds—The area within the sidelines and endlines of the court.

Intentional Foul—A deliberate foul generally committed near the end of the game to stop the clock, or in the hope that the fouled player will miss his free throws, and the defensive team will gain possession of the ball.

Jump Ball—The procedure used to put the ball in play at the beginning of a game or after a held ball. Two opponents face each other from either side of the free-throw line or the midcourt line. The referee tosses the ball up between the two opposing players, and they each jump up and attempt to tip the ball to their respective teammates.

Jump Shot—The shot executed when the player jumps into the air and releases the ball at the height of his jump.

Keyhole or Key—The area including the free-throw line, the foul line, and the foul circle.

Lay-up—A shot taken close-in to the basket and which the shooter delivers to a target on the backboard.

Lead Pass—A pass delivered in front of the intended receiver so that he can continue his forward motion and receive the ball without breaking stride.

Man-To-Man—The type of defense played when one defensive player guards one offensive player, as opposed to a "zone" in which a player defends a particular area of the court.

Mismatch—A situation in which a tall player is guarded by a smaller player because of a missed defensive assignment, a switch, or simply because of his defensive assignment.

Offensive Foul—A personal foul committed by an offensive player.

One-and-One—The bonus shot awarded a foul shooter if he sinks the first free throw awarded him because of the commission of a one-shot foul.

One-on-One—The offensive and defensive action between opposing players.

Open Man—An offensive man free of his defender and in good shooting position.

Outlet Pass—A quick, long pass downcourt made by a defensive rebounder to start his team's offensive movement toward its goal.

Out-of-Bounds—The area on or outside of the sidelines or endlines. If the ball goes out of bounds its possession is lost by the team whose player last touched the ball.

Out-of-Bounds Play—The strategy used by a team to put the ball back in play after it has gone out of bounds.

Palming the Ball—A violation that occurs when a dribbler turns his wrist and hand as he dribbles the ball. When this infraction is whistled by the referee, possession of the ball is awarded to the defensive team.

Passing Lane—The path between a passer and a receiver.

Penetration—The ability of an offensive team or player to move in close to the basket.

Percentage Shot—A shot an offensive player has a good chance of hitting.

Peripheral Vision—The ability of a player to see shapes and movement of players and the ball when they are out of his direct line of vision. It allows him to observe what is happening in the 180 degree area in front of him without turning his head.

Personal Foul—Illegal physical contact inflicted on one player by another—slapping, hacking, charging, etc.

Pick—A maneuver in which an offensive player without the ball positions himself in such a way that he screens a teammate's defender, and his teammate can move freely to the basket with the ball, or move freely to an open area of the court to receive the ball.

Pivot—The act of turning on one foot by planting one foot (keeping the ball of the pivot foot in contact with the floor) and pushing off with the other.

Pivotman—The center.

Position—The area of the court occupied by a player. Good position is related to the effectiveness of scoring, rebounding, and playing defense.

Post—The position established by the pivotman. A high post would be a position established near the free throw line; a low post would be one established near the basket.

Push Off—To illegally use the hands to push or move an opponent out of the way.

Rebound—It is a missed shot that bounces off the rim or the backboard, or it is the act of gaining control of such a missed shot.

Rim—The basket's circular metal frame.

Roundball—(Hoops, B-ball) Nickname for basketball.

Run and Gun—A run and shoot offense.

Sag—Movement of a defense or a defender from one position or man to another position or man to better cover an offensive threat. For example, a player will *sag* from his man to help cover a man with the ball.

Save—To keep the ball from going out of bounds.

Screen—The maneuver executed when an offensive man without the ball establishes a stationary position and acts as a barrier from behind which the man with the ball can shoot.

Shot Clock—A clock that indicates the time left for shooting; in the NBA players have 24 seconds in which to shoot.

Sixth Man—The first substitute to come off the bench.

Slam Dunk—(Slam, Jam, Stuff) A forceful dunk.

Spot—A favorite area on the court from which a player shoots well.

Stall—The maneuver executed when a team slows the action of the game and freezes, or holds the ball and makes no attempt to score. Teams use it when they are leading a game and wish to control the game by running time off the clock.

Steal—The act of a defensive man legally taking the ball away from an opponent.

Steps—(Walking) Traveling.

Stutter Step—A quick movement by a player from one foot to the other made in an effort to fake out his opponent.

Swish—Scoring by putting the ball through the basket without touching the rim.

Switch—To change defensive assignments in the middle of play.

Tap in—A basket scored by tipping the ball in the basket off a rebound from the rim or backboard.

Team Foul—A foul charged to a team's quota for a period. When that quota is exceeded by one team, the other team is awarded a bonus shot on subsequent fouls.

Technical Foul—A penalty for abusive, uncalled for behavior on the court. It is also a penalty for certain violations of rules. It gives a free throw and possession of the ball to the opponent of the offender.

Ten-Second Rule—Rule requiring the team in possession to move the ball from the backcourt across the mid-court line and into the front court within ten seconds of taking the ball out of bounds. Failure to do so causes the offensive team to lose possession.

Three-Point Play—The situation in which a player gets fouled in the process of scoring a basket and is given the chance to score a third point on the free throw.

Three-second Violation—The infraction whistled when an offensive player remains in the free-throw lane for more than three consecutive seconds.

Tip-in—A quick follow-up shot made when a player taps the ball into the basket without first gaining control of it.

Touch—A good feel for shooting the basketball.

Trap—A situation where defensive players "double team" a player.

Traveling—(Steps, Walking) The infraction whistled when an offensive player takes more steps with the ball than is allowed by the rules.

Zone Defense—A defense played when players guard positions on the court instead of individual players.

INDEX AND NOTES

BASKETBALL COURT DIAGRAM

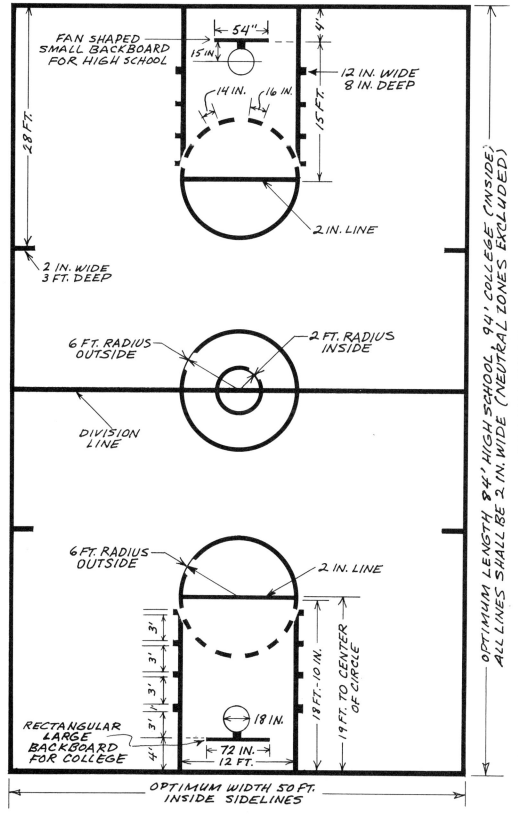

FAN SHAPED
SMALL BACKBOARD
FOR HIGH SCHOOL

54"

15 IN.

28 FT.

14 IN.   16 IN.

4'

15 FT.

12 IN. WIDE
8 IN. DEEP

2 IN. LINE

2 IN. WIDE
3 FT. DEEP

6 FT. RADIUS
OUTSIDE

2 FT. RADIUS
INSIDE

DIVISION
LINE

OPTIMUM LENGTH 84' HIGH SCHOOL, 94' COLLEGE (INSIDE)
ALL LINES SHALL BE 2 IN. WIDE (NEUTRAL ZONES EXCLUDED)

MINIMUM OF 3FT.

PREFERABLY 10 FT. OF UNOBSTRUCTED SPACE OUTSIDE.

6 FT. RADIUS
OUTSIDE

2 IN. LINE

3'   3'

3'

3'

3'

RECTANGULAR
LARGE
BACKBOARD
FOR COLLEGE

4'

18 IN.

72 IN.
12 FT.

18 FT.-10 IN.

19 FT. TO CENTER
OF CIRCLE

OPTIMUM WIDTH 50 FT.
INSIDE SIDELINES

NOTES

THE BACKBOARDS

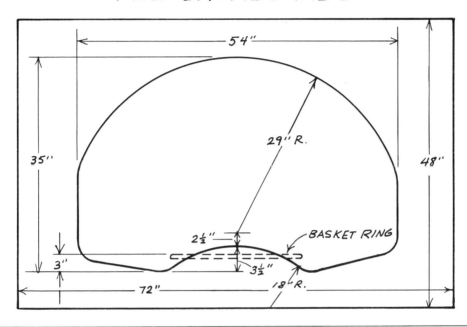

54"

35"

29" R.

48"

BASKET RING

2½"

3"

3½"

72"

18" R.

THE BALL

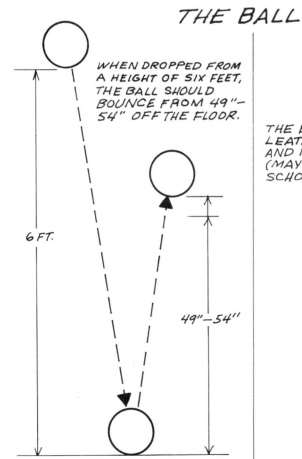

WHEN DROPPED FROM A HEIGHT OF SIX FEET, THE BALL SHOULD BOUNCE FROM 49"- 54" OFF THE FLOOR.

6 FT.

49"—54"

THE BALL MAY BE MADE OF LEATHER OR COMPOSITION AND IS 30" IN CIRCUMFERENCE (MAY BE 29" IN HIGH SCHOOL GAME.)

NOTES

NOTES

NOTES